RELIABLE
SOFTWARE
THROUGH
COMPOSITE
DESIGN

RELIABLE SOFTWARE THROUGH COMPOSITE DESIGN

Glenford J. Myers

VNR VAN NOSTRAND REINHOLD COMPANY
NEW YORK   CINCINNATI   ATLANTA   DALLAS   SAN FRANCISCO
LONDON   TORONTO   MELBORNE

Van Nostrand Reinhold Company Regional Offices:
New York   Cincinnati   Atlanta   Dallas   San Francisco

Van Nostrand Reinhold Company International Offices:
London   Toronto   Melbourne

Library of Congress Catalog Card Number: 74-19257
ISBN: 0-442-25620-6

Manufactured in the United States of America

Published by Van Nostrand Reinhold Company
135 West 50th Street, New York. N.Y. 10020

Published simultaneously in Canada by Van Nostrand Reinhold Ltd.

15 14 13 12 11 10 9 8 7 6 5 4 3 2 1

Library of Congress Cataloging in Publication Data

Myers, Glenford J   1946–
    Reliable software through composite design.

    Bibliography: p.
    1. Electronic digital computers—Programming.
I. Title.
QA76.6 M9   001.6'425   74-19257
ISBN 0-442-25620-6 pbk.

TO
the memory of my brother
David John Myers

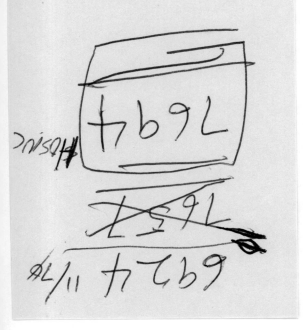

CONTENTS

PREFACE

Most computer programs are never designed; they are created on the coding pad. This practice leads to programs that are poorly constructed, resulting in higher production costs, higher maintenance and modification costs, and unreliability. Three categories of people are responsible for this problem: programming managers, educators, and programmers.

Most programming managers are overly "output oriented." Since code, the source language statement, is the largest part of the final product, they focus their attention on coding and divert attention away from the more important task, program design. Part of this approach is excusable, since design has traditionally been difficult to quantify, evaluate, and test.

Educators also are responsible for overemphasis on coding; many programming schools, classes, and texts teach only coding. Program designing is almost completely ignored.

Most programmers are unaware of good design strategies and techniques. Programmers and analysts who have discovered methodologies for program design have done little in trying to communicate this information to the remainder of the industry.

The purpose of this book is to begin solving this problem by defining a set of design measures, strategies, and techniques collectively known as *composite design*. This technology is used in the design of highly modular programs. By reducing a program's complexity, it has a positive effect on the program's quality and cost.

During the initial development of this book, the term *modular design* was used. However, several associates remarked that they had preconceived notions of modular design which they confused with the concepts in this book. There was another problem, too. Articles on modular programming appear frequently in many data processing periodicals, always preaching the benefits but rarely discussing techniques. People have stopped paying serious attention to literature in this area because they expect to read the same old story. To get around these problems, a new term, *composite design*, was chosen to represent the concepts in this book.

The first two chapters cover some background material, starting with an analysis of the current state of software design and development and proceeding through underlying concepts and definitions of composite design.

Chapters 3 and 4 discuss the two major measures of composite design, module strength and module coupling. Chapter 5 describes a set of additional, less important measures.

Chapters 6 and 7 are concerned with the "how" of design. As chapters 1 through 5 discuss the underlying design principles, chapters 6 and 7 discuss the methods of applying these principles. A technique called *composite analysis*, which is a problem-solving technique to turn a problem description into a program structure, is discussed.

Chapter 8 is concerned with the management of a programming project that includes composite design. It shows how to incorporate composite design into an overall programming process and also shows the relationship between composite design and other recently developed programming techniques. Chapter 8 also covers such other considerations as documentation and performance. Chapter 9 discusses the relationship of composite design and a virtual-storage environment. Chapter 10 describes a probabilistic model of program design with the intent of quantitatively measuring a design and predicting a program's stability. The Appendix defines a set of notation for describing program structures.

Although the book discusses theories of program design, its orientation is more toward the application of these theories. The material is oriented toward the experienced programmer or system analyst, not the beginning programmer. The concepts apply to both application program design and system program design and have been used in both environments.

The book is primarily intended as education and reference material for anyone faced with the task of designing a program (or anyone responsible for managing such an effort). It also would be useful as a text in a short course on program design or as a supplementary text in any university course on the design of programming systems.

Pertinent courses (based on the ACM curriculum recommendations) are:

Course UC4. Software Design.[7]
Course UD9. System Design and Implementation.[7]
Course C4. Software Design.[2]
Course D2. System Design.[2]
Course D3. Systems Development Projects.[2]
Course A8. Large-scale Information Processing Systems.[10]

I am indebted to Mr. L. L. Constantine, who contributed a number of ideas, particularly several of the strength and coupling measures in chapters 3 and 4 and part of the notation in the appendix.[8, 9] I am also indebted to those who were willing to study these ideas, use them, and supply me with feedback on the results. Special thanks are due Mr. D. T. Hooton and Mr. R. Eusebio for early acceptance of these ideas and helping me promote the ideas within IBM and to several IBM customers. I also thank Dr. N. Chapin for making several invaluable suggestions on the organization and content of the book.

CHAPTER 1

SOFTWARE DESIGN TODAY

Perhaps the biggest problem facing programming today is the extreme difficulty and cost of creating and maintaining large programming systems. An overused term, *modularity*, is often given as the answer to this problem.

To a large extent modularity, when interpreted correctly, *is* the answer.

> In particular, appropriate structuring of the system, its documentation, the project, its management, and all communication would greatly enhance maintainability and growth properities and extend the lifetime of large, complex programming systems.[4]

Note the word *appropriate* in this quotation; it is key to many concepts discussed later.

In the industry there is a lot of experience and knowledge, both published and unpublished, in the structuring of documentation, project organization, and project phases. A survey of the literature reveals that little thought has been given to the structuring of the system itself. A considerable amount (maybe too much) has been written on programming languages, coding, documentation, testing, and the like. Very little worthwhile information is available on the subject of program design.

This point is also illustrated in the recommendation made by a consulting firm to the United States Air Force about its programming environment:

> The single area which appears to offer the most promise for increased cost effectiveness is the area of design. There is a need for a formalized design process which can lead to both increased control of the project. . . . However, before this can be brought into effect on large projects it is necessary to expand and formalize our knowledge of programs and program structures.[19]

One obvious argument at this point is that a lot is known about programming. To a certain extent this is true. We're beginning to do a reasonable job of designing the external aspects of a program, namely languages, performance constraints, human factors, and file design. We're also fairly proficient in the actual programming of a well-defined function. For instance, when faced with the task of programming a subroutine to convert binary numbers into decimal numbers, most programmers would have little difficulty in flowcharting, coding, and testing this subroutine using one or more techniques for coding, testing, etc. Also, there is a lot of literature on the internal algorithms of a program or system—i/o buffering, paging, scheduling, sorting, memory allocation, and file searching.

To summarize, we know (in a relative sense) how to design the external aspects of a system, design the internal algorithms of a system, and design and code individual subroutines or programs within the system.

Note the missing link. How did we jump from the external specifications of the system down to the point where we were ready to begin designing internal algorithms and individual modules? This missing link, the subject of this book, is the design of the internal structure of the system.

THE DEATH OF A PROGRAM

The missing link is better illustrated by an example that describes a typical programming development effort. Suppose a rudimentary information-retrieval system is to be developed. The objective of the system is to retrieve the appropriate documents from a data base, given certain search criteria (keywords) specified by a user of the system. It will operate as an applications program, being multiprogrammed with other applications under the control of an operating system. The information-retrieval system communicates with a group of terminals and a data base of abstracts.

In the first step several systems analysts specify the external characteristics of the system. They specify the language seen by the terminal user, the data base design, and certain performance constraints, such as terminal response time and data base search time. The analysts go on to a second step, the internal design of the system. They design an algorithm to service the terminals and an algorithm to search the keywords in the abstracts. Then they hand their specifications to a programming group for implementation.

The programming group takes over, armed with a document containing specifications for the language, the file design, performance constraints, and several algorithms. They recognize that their first task is to define the modules in their system, since having a modular design is apparently a good trait. They regard this step very informally and as a nuisance, since it appears to be an obstacle to flowcharting and coding the system (what they consider to be the real work of a programmer). They perform this step using a combination of the following strategies:

Draw an overall flowchart of the system, making each block in the flowchart a module.

Create an initialization module because "every program has to have an initialization module." For the same reason they create a termination module, a control module, and several processing modules.

Assign each programmer an arbitrary piece of the system, allowing each person to work out his own structure.

Create a module to handle all input operations and another to handle all output operations.

Look for identical sequences of operations throughout the system, creating a module for each sequence.

Place many of the variables used in the program in a central global data structure, the Information Retrieval System Super Data Structure (IRSSDS).

Once this is done, the programmers sigh with relief and perform their "real work"—internal design, coding, testing, and (alas) debugging of each module. Finally, after several schedule slippages, a few design changes that unexpectedly affect almost every module, and some last-minute piecing and patching together, they get the system on the air.

Within a few months someone requests a modification of the program. That modification and each succeeding modification result in unexpected large internal changes. Finally, because the installation cannot afford paying a staff of programmers whose job is simply maintenance and modification of the system, the installation reluctantly stops all modifications. Now the static information-retrieval system cannot cope with the ever-changing needs of its users, so the users move elsewhere. End of a sad but typical tale.

The system died because no one recognized the need for appropriate structuring of the system. Also, as we will demonstrate later on, the six strategies listed are poor design strategies.

FACTS OF LIFE

The following generalizations about today's programming environment are for the most part obvious. However, it is worthwhile to analyze each one in respect to their ramifications on the business.

1. Programs Have Long Lives.

The popularity of emulators on today's third-generation systems illustrates the fact that programs die hard. Programs written 10 to 15 years ago are still in operation. Another illustration is the number of releases or versions of programming products. For instance, IBM's OS/360 has had more than 21 official releases. Its smaller brother, DOS/360, has had even more. IBM's OS/VS operating systems are largely based on code written for the earlier OS/360.

As a corollary, we can say that programs never achieve stability. They never achieve freedom from bugs or from additions or from changes.

2. Programmers Spend a Majority of Their Time Correcting Errors.

If you observe a cross section of programmers (even those developing new programs), you will find that most of their time is spent in testing, debugging, and correcting errors. It is not unusual for a large programming effort to have a six-month design phase, a six-month implementation (coding and unit testing) phase, and a 12-month testing phase. To the outsider it may seem that an operation that spends nine months on design and coding and 15 months on various levels of testing and debugging has its priorities backward. He is right!

3. TECHNICAL DECISIONS ARE OFTEN BASED ON PERSONAL PREFERENCES.

Decisions very often are made without considering alternatives and tradeoffs. I have heard programmers say, "To design a general and extendible system, data should reside in a set of flexible control blocks." This statement has no technical merit and, as I shall later show, is far from the truth. In fact, data should not reside in a set of flexible control blocks.

When two programmers debate alternatives, the decision is often based on emotional criteria such as who is louder or more persistent. This is partially justified because programming is still largely an art. However, building architecture is also considered an art. Why can't programmers debate in the same fashion that architects might debate? When architects argue over the material to be used for windows (tinted glass, tempered glass, plastic), they can substantiate their opinions with fact (for example, plastic is cheaper initially but has to be replaced every ten years because of discoloration from ultra-violet light). How often have you heard two programmers settle an argument based on an assessment of the alternatives in such terms as reliability, efficiency, cost, and clarity?

4. WE DON'T FOLLOW THE PRINCIPLE OF STANDING ON OTHERS' SHOULDERS.

> Perhaps the central problem we face in all of computer science is how we are to get to the situation where we build on top of the work of others rather than redoing so much of it in a trivially different way.[13]

When an electrical engineer designs a new television set, he doesn't design each vacuum tube, transitor, and capacitor from scratch; he relies on existing components. In fact, he normally designs on a much higher level, using off-the-shelf power supplies, oscillators, and other equipment.

In general, programming technologies today haven't advanced to this level. Furthermore, programmers aren't encouraged to operate in this mode. In the majority of new programming systems every single instruction is coded from scratch. In OS/360, for example, there are probably more than a hundred routines that have the function of converting a binary number to EBCDIC format. Furthermore, almost all of the routines probably work (although they're all implemented slightly differently), but a few of them probably contain some latent errors that haven't been detected yet.

5. THE DESIGN PROCESS OF DETERMINING THE MODULAR STRUCTURE OF A SYSTEM OR PROGRAM IS REGARDED VERY INFORMALLY.

The majority of project schedules do not consider design of the modular structure. Normally a nebulous step called *logic design* follows the external-specification step. Also, when a structural-design step *is* recognized, its significance is always overlooked. I have seen programmers criticize other programmers' external designs, detailed module designs, and code. I have never seen a module structure criticized.

6. A PROJECT OF 20 PROGRAMMERS NORMALLY HAS 20 UNIQUE SETS OF OBJECTIVES.

An interesting phenomenon is the manner in which people set objectives. Often, at the start of a project, objectives are stated for the program (what product is desired). These objectives usually state the expected external functions that the program should perform and, in some cases, the expected efficiency and reliability of the program.

So far so good. However, these are *program* or *product* objectives. A second set of equally important objectives, *project* objectives, is often overlooked. Project objectives cover factors of the design and such implementation processes as expected cost, elapsed project time, reliability, number of statements, core size, and quality of documentation. More importantly, since some of these factors oppose one another, project objectives direct the people designing and implementing the program on how to make the tradeoffs.

Because these objectives are almost never stated, the programmers on the project choose their own. One programmer may be trying to maximize reliability at any expense, and the next programmer may be trying to minimize core size at any expense. Weinberg has shown via experiments the variance in results that occur when programmers are aiming toward different objectives.[28]

7. SOFTWARE RELIABILITY IS NOW A LIFE-OR-DEATH MATTER.

A few years ago errors in software were publicized as causing refund checks to be written for $0.00. Today the situation is much more critical. Software errors have caused train crashes, the failure of a U.S. Mariner interplanetary flight, and a critical situation during the historic Apollo 11 landing. Software errors can also lead to false arrests, misappropriation of funds, invasions of privacy, lost merchandise, and shutdowns of businesses and factories that are highly dependent on their computing equipment.

The foregoing seven facts of life about the software business today lead to the following seven conclusions:

1. Because many programs live long lives (at considerable "medical" expense), the cost of extending or modifying programs is a key economic factor. This makes modifiability a significant attribute of a program.
2. Any mechanism that can decrease the cost of testing and debugging a large program is worth its weight in gold.
3. Objective means of evaluating the quality of a design and studying various alternatives are necessary.
4. The industry needs design and documentation techniques and management motivation to allow programmers to reuse the work of others instead of reinventing each new program instruction-by-instruction.
5. More rigor and management attention is needed in the program-design process.
6. Specific project objectives must be made clear to everyone at the beginning of every project.
7. Software reliability must improve significantly. This problem must be attacked on many fronts. Better design and implementation techniques are needed to reduce complexity and reduce unexpected side effects. Better testing techniques are needed to prove program correctness, to test all possible unique execution sequences, and to test programs in simulated environments.

The three principal factors in any programming effort are quality, cost, and time. A programming project is an optimization problem where we attempt to optimize one, two, or three of these factors subject to possible constraints on the other factors. For example, a typical programming project might have the goal of producing a program with maximum quality, but subject to constraints on cost (budget) and elapsed time (schedule). The ramifications of the cost and time factors are obvious enough to preclude further discussion. Program quality, on the other hand, needs further definition.

PROGRAM QUALITY

The factor of quality can be subdivided into factors of reliability, maintainability, modifiability, generality, usability, and efficiency. The major objective of composite design is the decomposition of the system or program into a set of highly independent pieces. Assuming for the moment that such decomposition techniques exist, we can see that they have a positive effect on program quality.

Reliability is a measure of the number of errors, or "bugs," encountered in a program. Composite design has a positive effect on reliability, since programs decomposed into highly independent pieces are less complex and the testing of such programs appears to be easier and much more straightforward.

Maintainability is a measure of the effort and time required to fix bugs in the program. Composite design has a significant effect on maintainability since errors can be isolated quickly and the fixes for errors are usually confined to only a small subset of the program.

Modifiability (or *extensibility* or *responsiveness*) is a measure of the cost of changing or extending the program. Composite design has a positive effect on modifiability. A program designed this way consists of highly independent pieces in which specific functions of the program are isolated from one another. Because of this, modifications to the program normally affect only a small subset of the parts. The "ripple effect," where a modification causes changes to ripple throughout the entire program, is minimized.

Generality is a measure of the scope of functions that a program performs. *Usability* is a measure of the human factors of a program. These factors are generally associated with the external characteristics of a program, so composite design has no known effect on these factors.

Efficiency is a measure of the execution behavior of a program —for example, in terms of execution speed and storage used. Composite design has no direct effect on a program's efficiency. Efficiency will be discussed further in chapter 8.

CHAPTER 2

CONCEPTS OF COMPOSITE DESIGN

One way of viewing any program is in terms of three basic attributes: function, performance, and structure. *Function* is a description of what a program does—the external characteristics of a program. *Performance* is a description of how well the program performs its functions, measured in such terms as execution speed, storage size, resource usage, and mean-time-to-failure. *Structure* is a description of the construction of a program, in such terms of coding structure, module structure, task (parallel-process) structure, memory layout, and module interfaces.

The intent of Figure 2.1 is to show the aspects of program design that composite design is concerned with. Composite design is concerned with the *structure* attribute of a program, in terms of module, data, and task structure and module interfaces. Composite design has no direct relationship with coding structures (the coding style within a module) or memory structures (the physical layout of a program within a memory). Composite design has no relationship with the function of a program (we assume the function has been determined prior to designing the structure). It also has no direct relationship with the performance of the program (although the program's structure could, in turn, affect its performance, particularly its reliability and execution speed).

Modularity is a popular term today. Often terms such as *modular* are added to the names of programs and to the titles of articles and books because "to be modular is to be good." Unfortunately, modularity is a widely misused and ill-understood concept. Within this book the word *modular* will be used to indicate a program that has

9

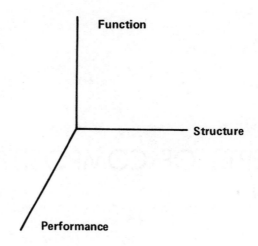

FUNCTION (what the program does)

    Purpose   Flexibility

    Generality   Human factors

PERFORMANCE (how well the program works)

    Speed   Reliability

    Size   Resource usage

STRUCTURE (how the program is constructed)

    Coding structure   Task structure

    Module structure   Memory structure

    Data structure   Interfaces

FIGURE 2.1. Program attributes

been structured into many highly independent parts, or modules.

The first order of business is to define the term *module*. For now we will not distinguish between "good" and "bad" modules but simply define the basic characteristics of a module. A module is a group of program statements with the following characteristics:

1. The statements are lexically together. That is, when viewing a listing of the statements, the statements are physically together on the listing.
2. The statements are bounded by identifiable boundaries (namely, START and END statements).
3. The statements are collectively referenced by a name (the module name).
4. The statements can be referenced, by the module name, from any other part of the program.

Therefore the module corresponds to structural entities in most languages, such as the subprogram and function in FORTRAN, the procedure in PL/I and ALGOL, the CSECT in OS/360 assembly language, and the subprogram in COBOL.

The purpose of a module (at least those modules containing executable statements) is to receive some input data, perform one or more transformations on the data, and return some output data. To depict this, the following form will be used to represent the use of a module:

CALL SQRT (A, B)

which means: Execute module SQRT, where the data named A and B are the input and output data.

Unless otherwise noted, the following assumptions will be made concerning modules:

1. When a CALL statement is executed, execution in this module is suspended until execution of the called module ends.
2. When execution of a module ends, execution resumes in the calling module. More plainly stated, all modules return to their callers.
3. When execution of a called module ends, execution of the calling module resumes with the statement immediately following the CALL statement.

Points 1 and 3 are simply popular conventions. Point 2 is a necessary condition in composite design.

BASIC NOTATION

Graphical notation plays an important part in composite design. The notation is illustrated in the Appendix. Figure 2.2 will be used

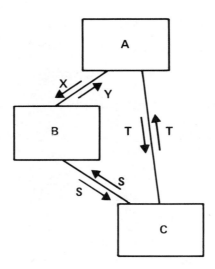

FIGURE 2.2. Notation

to explain the basics of the notation. The following information can be obtained from the figure:

1. There are three modules, A, B, and C.
2. Somewhere in module A there are at least two CALL statements, one for module B and one for C. A line leaving the bottom edge of a module and entering the top edge of another module represents a CALL.
3. Somewhere in module B, there is at least one CALL statement for module C.
4. B receives an input of X and returns an output of Y. C receives an input of S or T and passes S or T back as output, respectively. Arrows in parallel with module interfaces (CALLS) represent the parameters passed from one module to another and also indicate the usage of the parameters (i.e., input or output).
5. B is subordinate to A. C is subordinate to both A and B. Module N is subordinate to module M if module N is structurally below module M in the structural diagram.

Note that this type of diagram shows only structural relationships. It does not imply any procedural or algorithmic relationships. For instance, it does *not* tell us whether A calls B before it calls C, or vice versa, how many times A calls B, whether A calls B and C every time A is executed, and so on.

An alternate method for illustrating the parameters is shown in Figure 2.3.

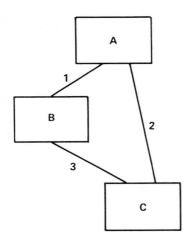

	In	Out
1	X	Y
2	T	T
3	S	S

FIGURE 2.3.   Describing interfaces

CONVENTIONS FOR PARAMETER NAMES

In most programming languages a parameter that is passed from one module to another can have two names—the name as defined in a calling module and the name as defined in the called module. For instance, a FORTRAN module A could contain the statement

CALL NUMBER (N)

and the called module could begin with the statement

SUBROUTINE NUMBER (IOTA)

The convention in the structure diagram is to use the parameter name as defined in the calling module. In this case the parameter would be known as N.

FUNCTION OF A MODULE

Every module has three basic attributes: function, logic, and interfaces. A key, and often misunderstood, definition is the *function* of a module. Understanding it is crucial to understanding composite design.

A module's function is the transformation (input to output) that occurs when the module is called. In other words, a module's function is "what happens when that module is called." A module's logic is the description of program flow within the module. (Discussion of module interfaces is deferred until Chapter 4.)

Although a module's function and logic are somewhat related, a clear distinction must be made between the two. This distinction is important because composite design is concerned primarily with the functions of modules within a program, rarely with the logic of the modules.

Note that the function of a module is related not only to the operations performed in that module, but also to the functions of any modules called by that module. When speaking of a module's function, the module should be viewed as a black box. That is, we shouldn't care how the module performs the function. In fact, we don't care whether the function is performed entirely within the module or whether the module calls other modules to perform the function.

To illustrate this, refer to Figure 2.4. The function of the top module in the program is to allocate an input/output device. The input to this module is probably a description of the type of device to be allocated, and the output is probably a description of the actual device allocated. We can see that very little of the logic to perform this function lies within this module. However, this has no bearing on the module's function.

Figure 2.5 is a second example. The function of the top module is to execute the next command. Again we see that little of the logic to do is this is actually in this module. In other words, we could have designed this part of a program as one large module or six modules as shown without altering its function.

A common mistake in Figure 2.5 would have been to define the function of the top module as a routing module. This would have been incorrect since routing describes logic, not function. In describing the function of a module, the following guidelines should be used:

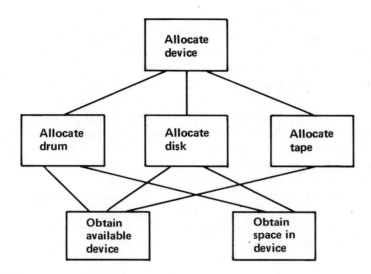

FIGURE 2.4.   Allocation program

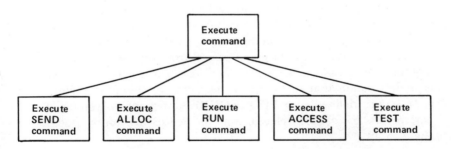

FIGURE 2.5.   Command processing

1. The function description must contain a verb. "Find password record" is a valid description; "password module" is not.
2. Avoid verbs that are ambiguous, such as *perform, process,* and *manage.* A function description such as "process master record" is nondescriptive.
3. Avoid words that denote logic such as *control, route,* and *interface.* "Control module" is a description of a module's logic, not its function.

OTHER DEFINITIONS

A *segment* is a group of statements having some of the characteristics of a module. The statements are lexically together, bounded, and may or may not have a collective name (segment name). Modules are comprised of one or more segments, which are either placed in the module originally or are copied into the module at compile time (for example, by the INCLUDE facility in PL/I). The concept of a segment is not used in composite design, although it is sometimes used in the later design and coding of individual modules (for example, structured programming).[20]

The *fan-out* of a module is the number of unique modules that are called from that module. In a structure diagram it represents the number of lines originating at the bottom edge of a module. For example, in Figure 2.3, the fan-out of module A is two. The *fan-in* of a module is the number of unique modules that call that module. In a structural diagram fan-in represents the number of lines entering the top edge of a module. In Figure 2.3 the fan-in of module C is two.

The *context* of a module is a particular usage of the module for a particular reason. For instance, a module whose function is "search string for a substring" might be used in two different contexts in a program: to search an input record for a particular transaction code and to search a line of text for a particular word.

An *argument* is a data name passed from one module to a called module (for instance, names in a CALL statement). A *parameter* is a data name that a module expects to receive (for example, in PL/I, names defined in a PROCEDURE statement). Arguments and parameters are closely related, and the words are often used interchangeably.

Throughout this book two terms are used, the *program* and the *problem*. The *program* is what we're designing; the *problem* is the reason for the program. The program is a solution to the problem (or class of problems).

THE KEY MEASURES

An important consideration in program design is having a set of objective measures of the design. With such a set of measures, the "goodness" or "badness" of a design can be objectively evaluated.

Module strength is a measure of the "goodness" of an individual module. *Module coupling* is a measure of the interconnections and relationships among modules.

For a better understanding of the importance of module independence and its relationships with module strength and module coupling, consider the following analogy: [1]

Consider a system of 100 lamps where a lamp could represent a statement or a segment in a program. Each lamp can be in one of two states, off or on. The lamps can be connected together in any fashion. If a lamp is on, the probability of its going off in the next second is 50 percent. If a lamp is off, the probability of its going on in the next second is 50 percent if at least one adjoining lamp is on. If a lamp is off, it will stay off as long as all of the lamps directly connected to (adjoining) it are off.

Consider the following three cases:

1. The 100 lamps are not connected at all to one another. The time to equilibrium (the time until all lamps go off permanently) is about seven seconds.
2. The 100 lamps are completely interconnected—that is, each lamp is connected to the other 99 lamps. In this system equilibrium is not reached until all 100 lamps happen to be off simultaneously. The time to equilibrium is 10^{22} years!
3. In the third case the lamps are partitioned into ten subsystems of ten lamps each. Within each subsystem the ten lamps are completely connected. However, the subsystems are independent of one another; there are no connections. The time to equilibrium is about 20 minutes.

Case 1 represents the ideal, but unreachable, extreme. No program can be composed of 100 completely independent parts. In any program all of its pieces have some relationship (however small) to one another. Case 2 represents the opposite extreme, where the 100 elements are completely intertwined. Case 3 represents a reasonable compromise, where the 100 lamps have been partitioned into 10 independent subsystems. Case 3 is slightly unrealistic since, as in case 1, a program cannot be subdivided into parts that are completely independent. However, as will be shown later, a situation close to case 3 can be achieved, which is a decomposition of a program into subsystems or modules, that are highly (but not completely) independent.

Looking at the times to equilibrium on a scale from case 1 to

case 2, case 3 approximates case 1. Assume that all lamps are off
and that, by some external means, a random lamp is turned on. The
incident of a lamp turning on is analogous to a modification of the
program (either due to the fixing of an error or a requested change).
The time to equilibrium is a measure of the stability of the system,
analogous to the extent of how a modification could ripple through
the program. A case-2 program might never achieve stability. A
case-3 program reaches stability quickly, and so in a case-3 program
changes are inexpensive and reliable.

Case 3 involves analyzing the system in some unspecified way
and decomposing the system so that relationships are maximized
within subsystems (module strength) and minimized among subsystems (module coupling). Chapter 3 concentrates on the idea
of module strength, that is, designing modules with maximum strength.
Chapter 4 discusses module coupling.

MODULE STRENGTH

The optimal modular design is one in which the relationships among elements not in the same module are minimized. There are two ways of achieving this: minimizing the relationships among modules and maximizing relationships among elements in the same module. These two methods are complementary and are used together. Module coupling is used to minimize the relationships among modules. Module strength is used to maximize the relationships among elements in individual modules.

The second method, maximizing relationships among elements in the same module, is the subject of this chapter. *Element* in this sense means any form of a piece of the module, such as a statement, a segment, or a subfunction. Any program has certain relationships among all of its elements. The basic intent of module strength is to organize these elements so that closely related elements fall into a single module and unrelated elements fall into separate modules.

The measure of module strength is one of the most important measures of a modular design. The scale of strength, from highest to lowest, is: functional, informational, communicational, procedural, classical, logical, and coincidental. This scale is not linear. Functional strength and informational strength are much stronger than all the rest, and the last three are much weaker than all the rest.

In the following pages each type of strength will be defined, illustrated in one or more examples, and rationalized as to why it is found at its particular position on the scale. The examples should show that high module strength has a positive effect on programming cost and on program quality (in terms of reliability, extensibility, and maintainability).

COINCIDENTAL STRENGTH

Coincidental strength occurs when there are no meaningful relationships among the elements in a module. Coincidental strength is usually the result of one of three situations: an existing program is modularized by splitting it apart into modules; modules are created to consolidate duplicate coding in other modules; or an existing program is broken up because of limitations in memory size.

As a simplistic example of the second situation, suppose the following sequence of instructions appears several times in a module or in several modules:

    A = B + C
    GET CARD
    PUT OUTPUT
    IF B=4, THEN E=0

A well-intentioned programmer may analyze the situation and decide to replace all such sequences with a CALL to module X, and then create a module X containing these four instructions.

Module X now probably has coincidental strength, since there are no apparent relationships among these four instructions. That is, these instructions probably have different meanings in the original modules.

Suppose in the future a need arises in one of the modules originally containing these instructions to say GET TAPERECORD instead of GET CARD. The programmer is now faced with a problem. If the instruction in module X is modified, module X is unusable by all of its other callers. He has another alternative, to place a test in module X to determine the calling module in order to decide whether to issue the GET TAPERECORD or GET CARD instruction. This alternative is equally bad.

It is only fair to admit that, independent of a module's strength, there are instances when any module can be modified in such a fashion to make it unusable by all its callers. However, the probability of this happening is very high if the module has coincidental strength.

LOGICAL STRENGTH

Logical strength, next on the scale, implies some logical relationship among the elements of a module. A logical-strength module is one that performs, at each invocation, one of a class of related functions. An example is a module that performs all input and output operations for the program or a module that edits all data.

The logical-strength "edit all data" module would probably be implemented as follows: Assume the data to be edited are master file records, updates, deletions, and additions. Parameters passed to the module would be the data along with a special parameter indicating the type of data. The first instruction in the module is probably a four-way branch, going to four sections of code: edit master record, edit update record, edit addition record, and edit deletion record.

As shown in Figure 3.1, these four functions are intertwined in some way in the module because the programmer took advantage of the fact that they exist in the same module. In the worst case the programmer coding the module could recognize that additions and updates are similar, so that in the update part of the module he branches to the additions part of the module, where he puts some code to determine whether or not to return to the update code. In the best case the code is still intertwined, perhaps simply because the four functions share the same data areas. In any event, the programmer maintaining this program is faced with an undesirable situation. If the deletion record changes and requires a change to the edit-deletion-record function, he probably has a problem, since this function is intertwined with the other three.

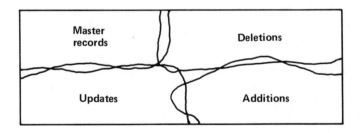

FIGURE 3.1. Module EDIT ALL DATA

In short, logical strength usually results in tricky code, intertwining of function that makes the program difficult to modify, a single interface for multiple functions, and the passing of unnecessary parameters (e.g., function codes). These last two points are discussed further in Chapter 4.

CLASSICAL STRENGTH

Classical strength is the same as logical strength, except that the elements are also related in time. Thus a module with classical strength performs a class of functions where the functions are also related in time.

The best examples of modules in this class are the traditional initialization, termination, housekeeping, and clean-up modules. Elements in an initialization module are logically related because initialization represents a logical class of functions. In addition, these elements are related in time since the elements are executed together, sequentially in time (at initialization time). Figure 3.2 is a flowchart of a classical-strength module.

Modules with classical strength tend to exhibit all of the disadvantages of strictly logical-strength modules. However, classical modules are higher on the scale since they tend to be simpler. All of the elements are usually executed at one time, since there are no parameters and logic to determine which elements to execute.

Classical-strength modules also tend to have a close relationship with other modules in the program. For instance, a module "initialize symbol table" has an obvious relationship with a module "add entry to symbol table." Consequently classical-strength modules are not highly independent modules. Also, classical-strength modules, because they perform a set of very specialized functions, are generally unusable in different contexts in the program or in different programs.

The question as to how to fit initialization and termination processing into a program structure is discussed in Chapter 5.

Certain types of classical-strength modules are sometimes unavoidable. One common example is a module whose functions involve "recovering" the program. For instance, a module whose functions are "after exception, diagnose the exception, correct the error if possible, and continue execution" has classical strength. There is no way to design such a module to make its strength higher than classical strength.

PROCEDURAL STRENGTH

Procedural-strength modules perform more than one function where the functions are related in respect to the procedure of the problem. Procedural-strength modules are often the result of flow-

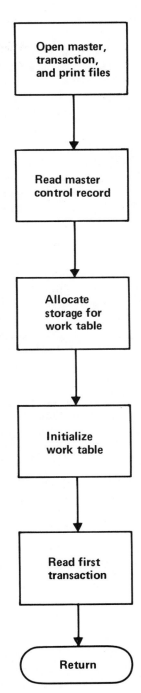

FIGURE 3.2.   Classical-strength module

23

charting the problem to be solved and then defining modules to represent one or more blocks in the flowchart.

Procedural-strength modules are similar to classical-strength modules except that the functions in a procedural-strength module are related to the procedure of the problem, while the functions in a classical-strength module are generally just lumped together because they must be performed at the same time. For instance, the module "zero summary table and mount next transaction tape" has classical strength, but the module "plot graph R2 on plotter and print report XYZ" has procedural strength.

Looking at it another way, classical-strength modules perform functions that are related to program procedure, not problem procedure. For instance, the function "zero summary table" would never appear in the problem description of an inventory-control problem. Because the functions in a procedural-strength module are related to the problem procedure, they tend to have a closer bond. Consequently procedural-strength modules have a greater degree of independence.

Procedural strength, although higher on the strength scale because of a close relationship to the problem structure, is still far from the ideal, which is functional strength. The reason is that the procedural processes in a program are usually distinct from the functions in a program. Hence a procedural-strength module can contain several functions or just part of a function. Such a module is difficult to use in other contexts. For instance, assume a module exists with the function "skip to the top of the next page and read next record." If, in another context, only the function "skip to the top of the next page" is needed, the tendency might be to modify this module to change its function to "skip to the top of the next page and/or read next record." This is undesirable for two reasons: First, the module had to be modified; second, its strength was reduced to logical strength.

COMMUNICATIONAL STRENGTH

A module with communicational strength is a module with procedural strength and an additional characteristic—all of the elements "communicate" with one another. That is, the elements in the module either reference the same set of data or they pass data among themselves: for example, the output of one element is the input of another element.

Consider the following modules:

A. Update record in data base and record the record in audit trail
B. Calculate new trajectory and send it to terminal
C. Update record in data base and read next transaction

Module A has communicational strength, since the elements use a common set of data (the record). Module B also has communicational strength, since the output of the first element (the trajectory) is the input to the other element. Module C has procedural strength, since the elements do not process the same piece of data.

Communicational strength is higher on the scale than procedural strength since the elements in a module with communicational strength have a stronger bond. That is, not only are they procedurally related, but they reference the same data. Because of this, communicational-strength modules tend to be more independent from other modules and to be more reusable in different contexts.

By now you may have observed that a module can have the characteristics, in part or in whole, of more than one strength. If a module totally exhibits several types of strengths, it is classified by the higher strength. For instance, a module with communicational strength also has, by definition, procedural strength. However, it is classified by the higher strength, communicational strength.

A module that partially exhibits several strengths is classified according to the lower strength. For instance, if a module has three elements, all of which are procedurally related and two of which use the same data, the module has procedural strength. A module with part classical strength and part procedural strength (for example, "read all input transactions and all master records and then print report headings") is classified with the lower strength, classical strength.

The next highest strength on the scale is informational strength. However, because it represents a variation of functional strength, discussion of informational strength will be deferred until later.

FUNCTIONAL STRENGTH

Functional strength is at the top of the strength scale. In a functional-strength module all of the elements are related to the performance of a single function.

A question that always arises at this point is, what is a function? In mathematics $y = f(x)$ is read "y is a function f of x." The function

f defines a transformation, or mapping, of the independent (or input) variable x into the dependent (or output) variable y. Hence a function describes a transformation from some input data to some output data. In terms of programming this definition is expanded to allow functions with no input data and functions with no output data.

In practice the above definition does not clearly describe a functional-strength module. One hint is that if the module does not fit the descriptions of the other types of strength—informational, communicational, procedural, classical, logical, coincidental—it has functional strength. If the elements of the module all contribute to accomplishing a single goal, then it probably has functional strength.

Examples of functional-strength modules are "compute square root," "obtain random number," "write record to output file," and "delete record from master file."

The first module, "compute square root," is a function with an input and an output (square root of the input). The second module, "obtain random number," is a function with an output but no input. The last two, "write record to output file" and "delete record from master file," are functions with an input parameter but no output parameter.

It is possible to form the impression that functional-strength modules represent only the primitive functions in a program (for example, "compute square root" is a primitive function). However, this impression is incorrect. Any module that performs a single function has functional strength even if it has many subordinate modules (implying that this function has been decomposed into a hierarchy of subfunctions). Such modules as "compile next source program," "execute EDIT command," "search data base for matching abstract," and "allocate i/o device" are certainly not primitive functions, yet each of them has functional strength.

INFORMATIONAL STRENGTH

The remaining type of module strength is informational strength. Although informational strength falls between communicational strength and functional strength, discussion of it has been deferred until now because it is closely related to functional strength.

A module with informational strength performs multiple functions where the functions, represented by entry points in the module, deal with a single data structure. In other words, this module represents the physical packaging together (into one module) of two or more modules having functional strength.

Consider the two functional-strength modules "insert entry into symbol table" and "search for entry in symbol table." These two modules deal with a single data structure, the symbol table. These two modules could be packaged into a single module (having informational strength) with two entry points, where the entry points represent the two functions. This is a desirable situation because knowledge of the symbol table is now buried in a single module, and if the symbol table format must be changed, only a single module must be changed. Informational strength is based on the idea of "information hiding," which is the isolation of knowledge of a data structure to a single module.[25]

There's an apparent contradiction here, since this example shows that informational strength is an improvement over functional strength, yet informational strength is below (but close to) functional strength on the strength scale. The reason is that informational strength is more difficult to deal with and thus the chance for error is greater. Because multiple functions have been packaged into one module, the opportunity to intertwine these functions exists, even if they weren't intertwined when they were initially coded. An informational-strength module can easily have all of the disadvantages of logical strength, unless great care is taken to make sure that the coding of each function is independent from the other functions in the module.

To be categorized as an informational-strength module, a module must meet all of the following criteria: it must perform multiple functions, each function must be represented by an entry point in the module, each entry point must have the characteristics of a module with functional strength, and all of the functions must perform some transformation on the same data structure. An informational strength module is represented as shown in Figure 3.3.

There appears to be another possible implementation of an informational-strength module. Instead of multiple entry points, the module has a single entry point with a "function code" in the input parameters, which indicates which function should be executed. A module with this characteristic has logical strength, not informational strength. This implementation is undesirable for three reasons. First, the code of each function is somewhat more intertwined, because the module probably starts with an *n*-way branch, based on the function code. Second, the module has a single interface for multiple functions, which is undesirable because which parts of the interface are pertinent to which functions must be documented. Also, a module that calls

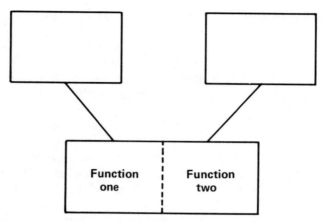

FIGURE 3.3.   Informational-strength module

this module to perform only one of the functions will probably have to be aware of the other functions (because of the single interface). Third, an interface with function codes represents "control coupling" (see chapter 4).

CATEGORIZING MODULES

A useful technique in determining the strength of a module is writing a sentence describing the function (purpose) of the module and then examining the sentence. The following tests can be made:

1. If the sentence is a compound sentence, contains a comma, or contains more than one verb, the module is probably performing more than one function; therefore it doesn't have functional strength. If the sentence has more than one verb and the verbs are connected by *or*'s, then the module probably has logical strength. If the verbs are connected by *and*'s, then the module may have classical, procedural, or communicational strength.
2. If the sentence contains words relating to time, such as *first, next, then, after, when,* and *start,* then the module probably has procedural strength.
3. If the predicate of the sentence doesn't contain a single specific object following the verb, the module probably has logical strength. For example, "edit all data" has logical strength; "edit source statement" has functional strength.

4. Words such as *initialize* and *clean-up* imply classical strength.

In some instances you may have difficulty in matching a module to the definitions of the categories of strengths. If this occurs, try determining what disadvantages your module has and then locate the strength category with the matching set of disadvantages.

Figure 3.4 represents a structural diagram of a program. The purpose of the program (i.e., the function of the "top" module) is to update a customer file. Input to the first module is a customer record (for example, number, name, address, status, and data on sales). The customer file contains customer records. Each customer record is followed by any number of sale records, which contain data on sales to that particular customer. The program will create a new customer record or update an existing customer record.

Try to analyze the modules and determine their strength. Your results can then be compared with the following analysis.

The analysis of this structure follows:

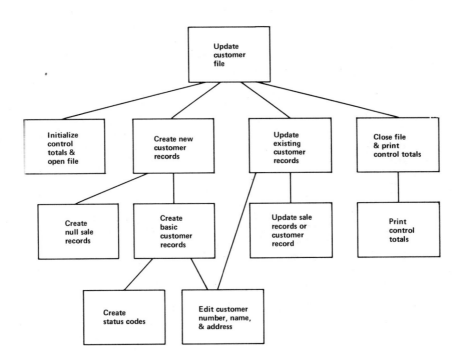

FIGURE 3.4.   Account program

1. Module INITIALIZE CONTROL TOTALS AND OPEN FILE has classical strength.
2. Module UPDATE SALE RECORDS OR CUSTOMER RECORD has logical strength since it performs a class of logically related functions (updating records).
3. Module CLOSE FILE AND PRINT CONTROL TOTALS has classical strength. Although the element "print control totals" is procedurally related to the problem, the other element, "close file," is not. Consequently the module has classical, not procedural, strength.
4. Module EDIT CUSTOMER NUMBER, NAME, AND AD-DRESS may, at first glance, appear to have logical strength. However, it actually performs a single function but on three specific pieces of data. Therefore, this module has functional strength.
5. The other modules appear to have functional strength.

As we moved up the strength scale, several effects should have been observed. The bond between the elements of the module increased as the strength increased. This tends to increase the reliability of the program because strong modules have more independence (the bonds are within a module, not across modules). Extensibility and maintainability are higher because changes to the program are isolated to a small subset of its parts. Stronger modules are more usable in different contexts and in other programs because they tend to be less specialized.

Figure 3.5 is a decision table that can be used as an aid in determining the strength of a module. Blank boxes in the top half of the table represent "don't care" conditions. Table 3.1 summarizes the attributes of each type of strength.

Table 3.1   Strength Attributes

Strength	Independence from Other Modules	Suscepti-bility to Errors	Usability in Other Programs	Extensibility
Functional	High	Low	High	High
Informational	High	Medium	High	High
Communicational	Medium	Low	Medium	Medium
Procedural	Medium	Low	Low to medium	Medium
Classical	Low	Medium	Low	Medium
Logical	Medium	High	Medium	Low
Coincidental	Low	Very high	Low	Low

Difficult to describe the module's function(s)	Y	N	N	N	N	N	N	N
Module performs more than one function			Y	Y	Y	Y	Y	N
Only one function performed per invocation			Y	N	N	N	Y	
Each function has an entry point			N				Y	
Module performs related class of functions		N	Y	Y				
Functions are related to problem's procedure				N	Y	Y		
All of the functions use the same data					N	Y	Y	
Coincidental	X	X						
Logical			X					
Classical				X				
Procedural					X			
Communicational						X		
Informational							X	
Functional								X

FIGURE 3.5.   Determining strength

31

CHAPTER 4

MODULE COUPLING

There are two major measures of modularity. The first, module strength, described in the previous chapter, is a measure of the relationships among the internal elements of a module. The second measure, coupling, is a measure of the relationships among modules.

Coupling is the second measure of the independence of modules. Since a highly modular design is achieved by maximizing the relationships among the elements of a module and minimizing the relationships among modules, the scale for coupling is inverse to the scale for strength. Thus the goal is achieving high strength and low coupling.

Figures 4.1 and 4.2 represent a five-module program. In Figure 4.1 the coupling is high, since every module is coupled to every other module and the degree of coupling is high (as indicated by the heavy lines). Figure 4.2 represents a much better structuring of the program. Interconnections among modules have been minimized, as well as the degree of each interconnection.

The scale of coupling, from lowest coupling (best) to highest (worst), is data coupling, stamp coupling, control coupling, external coupling, common coupling, and content coupling. Following the pattern of the previous chapter, this chapter will define each type of coupling, give one or two examples, and explain why it sits where it does on the scale.

CONTENT COUPLING

Two modules are content coupled if one module makes a direct reference to the contents of the other module. This occurs in the following situations:

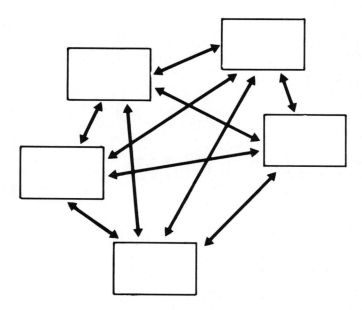

FIGURE 4.1.   High coupling

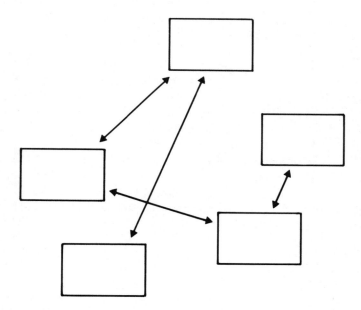

FIGURE 4.2.   Loose coupling

1. One module modifies a program statement in another module.
2. One module refers to nonexternally declared data in another module. An example of nonexternally declared data is a data element in a PL/I module that does not have the EXTERNAL attribute. Thus a reference to data in another module where the symbolic name of the data was not resolved by a preprocessor, such as a linkage editor, implies content coupling.
3. One module branches into another module. The statement to which it branches is not defined as an external entry point.
4. Two modules share the same contents. This can occur when the statements of one module lie physically within another module or when two modules physically reside in one compilable entity (for example, two CSECTS in the same "module" in OS/360 assembly language).

It should be obvious that content-coupled modules are very dependent upon one another and that a seemingly innocent change in one module can easily cause the other module to malfunction.

In situations 1, 2, and 3 above, one module is dependent on actual displacements within the second module. Almost any change to the second module will require a change to the first module. Also, a significant change in one module, such as the use of a new algorithm or a change in data attributes or format, may require an extensive design change of the entire program.

Although situation 4 does not necessarily imply situation 1, 2, or 3, we can show that it sets up a very good "ambush" to allow the programmer to easily create situation 1, 2, or 3. Suppose that two modules, READ-FROM-TERMINAL and WRITE-TO-TERMINAL, are created and exist in one compilable entity. Suppose, also, that they started out containing two unique sets of program statements and data.

At a later point in time, while a programmer is modifying the input/output statements in the two modules, he notices that most of the input/output statements in the two modules are identical. In a move to economize he removes the statements from one module and simply branches into the other module as shown in Figure 4.3. (He can easily do this because they were both in the same compilable entity.)

So far the two modules still operate correctly, but they are tightly coupled. Now a new programmer is asked to change module WRITE so that it writes some data to an audit trail before it writes to the terminal. He writes a WRITE-AUDIT-RECORD module and, upon

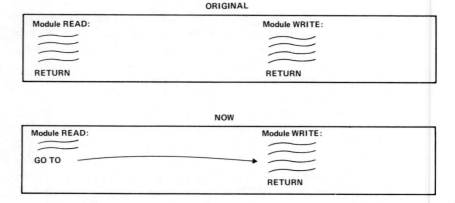

FIGURE 4.3.   Content coupling

examining module WRITE, inserts a CALL instruction as shown in Figure 4.4.

He has now created a bug in the program, since the execution of module READ now also causes an audit record to be written.

Although this example may appear to be trivial, it shows that content coupling has an important fault. Content coupling has a negative effect on the clarity of a program and therefore causes changes to the program to be unreliable. If a program contains content coupling, it is difficult to make an isolated modification to the program without inspecting the logic of the entire program to determine the ramifications of the content coupling. In a large program this detailed inspection may not be feasible, making modifications of the program a risky task.

Fortunately, certain programming languages discourage the use of content coupling. If a program is coded in an assembly-level language, the four situations of content coupling can occur. Coding in a higher-level language discourages the first three situations.

When two or more modules are packaged together, content

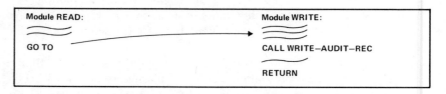

FIGURE 4.4.   A bug

coupling is not always present. However, content coupling in this situation can be very subtle; for instance, it can be caused by the sharing of a data area. Functions in an informational-strength module are, by definition, content coupled. All informational-strength modules should be examined to ensure that the content coupling is due to the sharing of a single data structure, not due to the sharing of code.

COMMON COUPLING

A group of modules are common coupled if they reference a shared global data structure (a common environment). The term *common environment* is named after the COMMON statement in FORTRAN and is a central repository for data elements. Three examples of this are a set of data elements with the EXTERNAL attribute that is copied into PL/I modules via an INCLUDE statement, data elements defined on the COMMON statement in FORTRAN modules, and a centrally located control block or set of control blocks.

Common coupling causes three weaknesses in the modules that are common coupled. First, a modification of only several modules may impact every module that is common coupled to these modules. For instance, assume only two modules reference a data element X in the common environment. We desire to expand X from two bytes in length to four bytes. The necessary changes are made to the two modules, but then we discover, to our dismay, that every module that references the common environment must be recompiled.

As a second example, assume a 20-module program exists and each module contains the PL/I statement:

% INCLUDE PDATA;

which instructs the compiler to copy the following global data into each module:

```
DCL 1 PDATA EXTERNAL,
        2 VENDOR  FIXED,
        2 CATEGORY CHAR(4),
        2 INVOICE,
        2 ISSDATE CHAR(8),
        2 MATCH FIXED BINARY,
        2 DRIVER CHAR(8);
```

Now a need arises to change CATEGORY from CHAR(4) to CHAR(6). Even though CATEGORY may be used by only a few modules, the entire 20 modules must be recompiled in order to give the compiler the new offsets of INVOICE and the variables following it.

In OS/360 most of the operating system's data elements are contained in system control blocks. These control blocks are mapped, element by element, in mapping macros. Any module that references a data element must contain the mapping macro of the proper control block. Anyone familiar with the ongoing development and maintenance of OS/360 knows that the "macro problem" is a very costly one. Since the mapping macros are constantly changing, and since it is not feasible to recompile the many thousands of modules in the system whenever a macro changes, the modules always contain varying versions of the same macro. This has led to more bugs in OS and also to costly procedures to attempt to track and control this situation.

The second weakness is explained as follows: A desirable goal is limiting the references in each module to only those data elements that the module is supposed to reference. With common coupling this is impossible, since each module can potentially reference every data element in the common environment. This leads to future problems in modification of these modules. For instance, when modifying a module, the programmer may decide to add a reference to another data element in the common environment. This can lead to bugs in such instances as (1) the other modules that use this data element assume that they were the only users or (2) the programmer uses the data element for other than its intended purpose. In general such modifications cause the data references in the program or system to become unstructured, uncontrolled, and often unknown.

Again OS/360 can be used as an example. OS has a large data structure—called the communications vector table—in a well-known location in its memory. Almost every data element in the system can be located via the CVT. Hence every module in OS is potentially common coupled. This has added cost to OS in trying to keep track of, and control, which modules reference which data elements.

A third weakness is that if a module references a common environment, it is difficult to use that module elsewhere in the program or in another program.

Assume that in a payroll program there is a module named COMPFICA. COMPFICA computes an employee's F.I.C.A. deduction, using the salary as an input parameter and obtaining this year's F.I.C.A. rate from the common environment. We now need to modify the payroll program, adding a function to compute, for the next year, the week when an employee's F.I.C.A. deductions will terminate. We desire to use COMPFICA with next year's F.I.C.A., but we face a possible problem, since if we temporarily modify the F.I.C.A. element in the common environment, we may cause a problem in some other part of the program.

Attempting to use a common-coupled module in another program, one without such a common environment, is very difficult. Generally there are two alternatives: scrapping the idea and writing a new module or creating a "fake" common environment before calling the module. The former is costly, since we are "reinventing the wheel." The latter leads to complex and cumbersome coding.

Although common coupling is undesirable, the disadvantages of common coupling become less severe if the common environment is limited to a subset of the modules in a program. If common coupling cannot be avoided, it is desirable to limit access to the common environment to a minimal subset of modules. This tends to lower the overall coupling in the program. Furthermore, it is desirable to limit access to the common environment to the "top" modules in the structure, since this still removes the disadvantages of common coupling from the "lower" modules in the structure (for example, allowing them to be used in other programs).

Common coupling has been discussed in detail because its use is widespread today. Many critics feel that common coupling leads to generalized designs. However, there is no objective proof of this and the only indications available lead us to believe that common coupling leads to costly and nonextensible designs. Fortunately, the weaknesses of common coupling are beginning to be recognized. For instance, in a paper on program maintenance and growth Belady and Lehman made the following observations:

> These concepts reflect the accepted viewpoint that a well structured system, one in which communication is via passed parameters through defined interfaces, is likely to be more growable and require less effort to maintain than one making extensive use of global or shared variables.[4]

EXTERNAL COUPLING

Two modules are external coupled if they both reference the same externally declared symbol. External coupling is similar to common coupling except that, in external coupling, the references between modules are to individual data items, not to data structures. For instance, a PL/I module referencing a symbol with the EXTERNAL attribute, an APL function (module) referencing a global variable, or an IBM S/370 assembly language module containing a "V-constant" are externally coupled with other modules (the modules containing or referencing the symbol).

Consider the case in Figure 4.5. GETCOMM is a module whose function is getting the next command from a terminal. In performing this function GETCOMM calls the module READT, whose function is to read a line from the terminal. READT requires the address of the terminal. It gets this via an externally declared data element in GETCOMM called TERMADDR. READT passes the line back to GETCOMM as an argument called LINE. If READT was coded in PL/I, it would begin with the following two statements:

READT: PROCEDURE (LINE);
DECLARE TERMADDR CHAR(8) EXTERNAL;

Note the arrow extending from inside GETCOMM to inside READT. An arrow of this type is the notation for externally declared references.

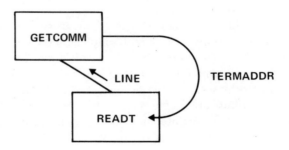

FIGURE 4.5. External coupling

So far so good. Now, however, a change must be made to this program. A module called GETDATA will be created, and its function is to get the next data line (not a command) from a terminal. The person making this modification recognizes that it would be desirable to use the module READT as a subroutine of GETDATA. There are at least five alternative designs, which are examined below.

1. GETDATA calls READT. Before it calls READT, it modifies TERMADDR so that READT has the intended terminal address,

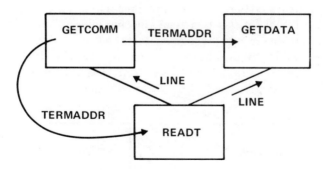

FIGURE 4.6.   Trying to add a new module

as shown in Figure 4.6. Note that a bug has probably been
created. GETCOMM, as originally coded, never knew that any
other module would change TERMADDR. Therefore, when
GETCOMM executes after GETDATA, GETCOMM will be
using the wrong terminal.

2. If the programmer of GETDATA recognized this problem, he
   might put instructions in GETDATA to save the current value
   of TERMADDR, set TERMADDR, call READT, and then
   restore the original value of TERMADDR. However, if there is
   a chance that GETDATA and GETCOMM can execute simultaneously (for instance, in a multiprogramming environment),
   then the bug still exists. Even if there isn't such a possibility,
   this code can be classified as tricky and thus subject to future
   error.

3. The programmer of GETDATA might recognize the problem
   and decide to modify GETCOMM. He changes GETCOMM so
   that it reinitializes TERMADDR each time it calls READT. This
   may eliminate. the bug, but consider the cost. The programmer
   of GETDATA had to modify GETCOMM, a module that should
   have been independent of GETDATA. Again, if GETDATA and
   GETCOMM can execute simultaneously, then a bug still exists.

4. The programmer of GETDATA might anticipate the above cases
   and decide that the easy way out is to code his own read line
   function, either within GETDATA or as another new module.
   This is unfortunate because by not using the existing READT
   module he is in effect reinventing the wheel. In addition the
   program now has two read line functions. This is undesirable
   for two reasons: first there is additional cost (two almost identical functions have been coded), and second, if the terminal

characteristics change, the programmer making the change must remember that he has two read line modules to change.

5. The programmer may recognize that the real problem is high coupling and may decide to correct it by lowering the coupling. As shown in Figure 4.7, he makes TERMADDR an input argument to READT instead of an externally declared data item.

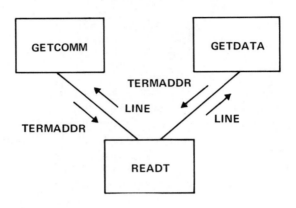

FIGURE 4.7.   Removing external coupling

In the long run alternative 5 is best, although it is also costly, since both GETCOMM and READT had to be modified.

This simple example shows that external coupling has an adverse effect on program modification, both in terms of cost and potential bugs. If GETCOMM and READT were not externally coupled from the beginning—if TERMADDR were passed as an argument—the addition of GETDATA would have been much simpler.

A second type of external coupling is a reference to an externally defined statement within a module—for instance, when one module branches to an externally defined statement within another module. I leave it to the reader to convince himself that this is at least as bad as the case of externally defined data shown above.

External coupling and common coupling are closely related. The difference is that common coupling involves a dependence on the entire common environment, while external coupling involves a dependence on only individual variables in the common environment. In OS/360 the many modules that contain a map of the entire CVT data structure are all common coupled together. If an alternate approach had been used—such as placing external references in the modules only to those individual data items used by the individual modules—two positive results could have been achieved: (1) external coupling instead of common coupling (more module independence); (2) reduced scope of coupling—instead of all the modules being common coupled to one another, only those modules using the same data item would be coupled, and the coupling would look more like Figure 4.2 than Figure 4.1.

CONTROL COUPLING

Two modules are control coupled if one module passes elements of control as arguments to the other module. An element-of-control argument directly influences the execution of the called module. Typical elements of control are function codes, flags, and switches.

Control coupling is undesirable because the two modules are not very independent. Since the calling module influences the execution of the called module (and hence has some knowledge of the internal processing of the called module), the called module is not a "black box." An additional side effect sometimes occurs with control coupling; many times the strength of the called module is low, not functional strength.

The two modules in Figure 4.8 are control coupled because argument PARSE is a switch that instructs GETCOMM to return either a parsed or an unparsed command.

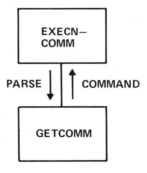

FIGURE 4.8.   Control coupling

A better structure is shown in Figure 4.9, where EXECNCOMM calls GETCOMM for an unparsed command or GETPCOMM for a parsed command.

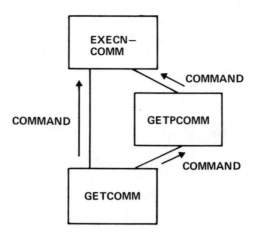

FIGURE 4.9.   Eliminating control coupling

A usual question at this point is, aren't there more program statements now in EXECNCOMM, or isn't EXECNCOMM more complex, since it calls *two* modules? In most cases the answer is no. In the first structure EXECNCOMM probably included a decision about whether or not to set PARSE before calling GETCOMM. The statement that set PARSE to "yes" can be removed and replaced with a call to GETPCOMM. In other words, the following code in EXECNCOMM

    PARSE = 0;
    IF NUCOMP = 'XYZ' THEN PARSE = 1;
    CALL GETCOMM (PARSE, COMMAND);

can be replaced with:

    IF NUCOMP = 'XYZ'
        THEN CALL GETPCOMM (COMMAND)
        ELSE CALL GETCOMM (COMMAND);

Hence EXECNCOMM is no more complex and contains no additional statements.

Control information also usually implies that additional "defensive" coding must be written. Consider a module whose function is "edit any transaction." The input parameters are the transaction, and a function code specifying what type of editing should be done. Code has to be written to determine if the function code is valid.

This extra coding could be avoided by eliminating the function code and replacing this logical-strength module with a set of functional-strength modules, as shown in Figure 4.10.

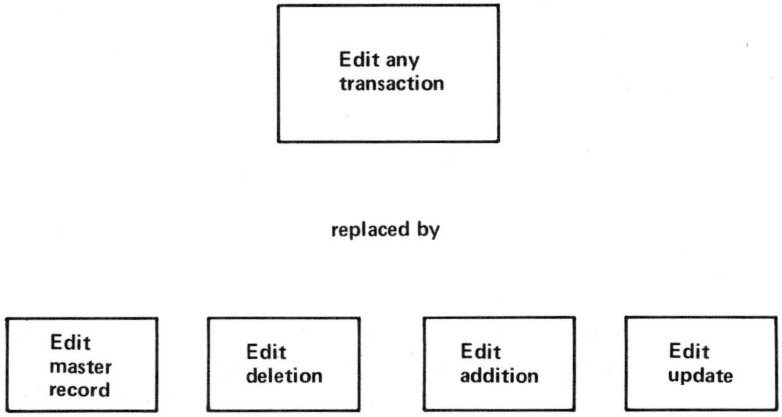

FIGURE 4.10.   Eliminating function codes

In addition to complicating the called module, control coupling can also complicate the calling module. The interface description in Figure 4.11 describes a single interface for three functions. Parameters P1 and P2 are elements of control.

```
CALL READ/WRITE (P1, P2, P3, P4, P5, P6, P7)
Parameters:
    P1:  Function code (read = 1, write = 2)
    P2:  Move/locate mode flag (move = 0, locate = 1)
         Locate is invalid if P1 = 2.
    P3:  Record (unused if read locate mode)
    P4:  Address of record (unused for read move mode
         and write)
    P5:  Length of record
    P6:  File name
    P7:  End of file indicator (unused for write)

    P1, P2, and P6 are inputs.
    P4 and P7 are outputs.
    P3 and P5 are outputs for read and inputs for write.
```

FIGURE 4.11.   Module READ/WRITE

A programmer coding a module that calls READ/WRITE to perform the read-move-mode function has to know about all three functions in order to figure out the interface. Also, this "one interface—multiple functions" interface can cause unnecessary modifications to modules in the program. Assume P6 is changing to allow a list of file names for read operations (for example, concatenated files). Modules calling READ/WRITE to perform only write functions now potentially have to change because of the common interface.

If READ/WRITE were replaced by three modules (one for each function), the design would be improved. Calling modules would not have to set function codes and mode flags. The interfaces would be more straightforward, as shown in Figure 4.12.

```
CALL READ/MOVE (P1, P2, P3, P4)
    P1:   File name (input)
    P2:   Record (output)
    P3:   Length of record (output)
    P4:   End of file indicator (output)

CALL READ/LOCATE (P1, P2, P3, P4)
    P1:   File name (input)
    P2:   Address of record (output)
    P3:   Length of record (output)
    P4:   End of file indicator (output)

CALL WRITE (P1, P2, P3)
    P1:   File name (input)
    P2:   Record (input)
    P3:   Length of record (input)
```

FIGURE 4.12.   Replacing module READ/WRITE

STAMP COUPLING

Two modules are stamp coupled if they reference the same data structure, providing that this data structure is not global (not in the common environment).

Stamp coupling is similar to common coupling. With common coupling, however, the data are globally defined to the system or program. With stamp coupling the data structure is not globally known. This implies that the name or location of the data structure is passed through the program as a parameter.

Assume that a PL/I-coded module contains an INCLUDE statement that generates a set of DECLARE statements mapping a large data structure. If this data structure has the EXTERNAL attribute, the module is common coupled to any other modules containing the same INCLUDE statement. If the data structure is passed to this module as an input parameter, the module is stamp coupled to any other modules referencing the data structure.

To examine the consequences of stamp coupling, first review the disadvantages of common coupling:

1. A seemingly isolated change in the data structure probably affects all modules that are common coupled together via this structure.
2. Common coupling clashes with the goal of trying to restrict a module's access to only the individual data items that it needs.
3. Because the data are globally known, it is difficult to use a common coupled module in different contexts in the program or in other programs.

Stamp coupling does not solve the problems, but it can reduce the effects of the last two. The second problem is less severe because access is given to one data structure, not necessarily the entire set of global data. The third problem is reduced because the program can handle multiple versions of the data structure. To understand this, consider the COMPFICA module discussed earlier. The module couldn't be reused in the program to compute next year's FICA because FICA in the common environment was this year's FICA. In this case COMPFICA probably contained such statements as:

```
DECLARE 1 DEDUC EXTERNAL,
          2 FEDRATE FIXED DECIMAL (4,4),
          2 STATRATE FIXED DECIMAL (4,4),
          2 FICALIM FIXED DECIMAL (7,2),
          2 FICA FIXED DECIMAL (4,4);
```

However, if DEDUC was not declared as EXTERNAL and if DEDUC was an input parameter to COMPFICA, then COMPFICA would be stamp coupled. COMPFICA could then be used to compute next year's FICA by building a temporary data structure, putting next year's rate in it, and passing the structure to COMPFICA.

All modules that reference the same data structure are stamp coupled with one another. For instance, module A, whose initial few statements are shown below, is stamp coupled with all of its callers and any other modules that reference the data structure N. In addition, all of A's callers are stamp coupled with one another.

```
A: PROCEDURE (M,N);
DCL M;
DCL 1 N,
       2 N1,
       2 N2,
          3 N21,
          3 N22;
```

As was pointed out in the previous chapter, stamp coupling can be eliminated in some situations by using informational-strength modules.

DATA COUPLING

Two modules are data coupled if one calls the other and they aren't content, common, external, control, or stamp coupled. In other words, all input and output to and from the called module is passed as arguments. Also, all of the arguments are data elements, not control elements or data structures.

A simple variable or a table of names where physical position in the table has no meaning imply data coupling. A data structure such as a data base record or an array where different rows have different meanings (for instance, the first row contains office totals and the second row contains region totals) imply stamp coupling.

Data coupling has the same relationship with stamp coupling that external coupling has with common coupling. Thus data coupling involves communication through the pertinent data items, not entire data structures. To illustrate this, consider the COMPFICA module again. When COMPFICA was stamp coupled, it was easier to use it in a different context (to compute next year's FICA). However, to do this, a DEDUC structure had to be built, filling in dummy (unused) fields such as FEDRATE and STATRATE in order to supply an accurate structure. If COMPFICA had been data coupled, this could have been avoided, since FICA and FICALIM themselves would be input parameters. In addition, COMPFICA's access would now be restricted to only the data it needs. COMPFICA doesn't need FEDRATE and STATRATE (income taxes). They were in the DEDUC structure because of needs elsewhere in the program. This points out that data coupling involves passing the pertinent data items as parameters, as opposed to passing potentially large structures of unneeded information (stamp coupling).

Data coupling is the lowest degree of coupling. Thus modules that are data coupled are highly independent. When data coupling is used, subordinate modules can be viewed as black boxes. That is, given an adequate description of its function and input and output parameters, there should normally be no reason to examine the insides of a subordinate module. If we're reading a program that is entirely data coupled and we encounter a statement in a module such as

CALL EXTRACT (A,B)

there should be no immediate reason to have to look at the code in module EXTRACT. However, if the program isn't entirely data coupled, we probably have to read the code in module EXTRACT to determine how the program works, since EXTRACT may require other implicit inputs or outputs (i.e., if it is external or common coupled). Hence, in addition to affecting the independence of a program, coupling also affects the readability of a program. If other than data coupling is used, the reader is forced to jump around from module to module in order to understand the logic of the program.

Programming languages could take an additional step to improve the readability of programs. The CALL statement above does not indicate how EXTRACT uses the arguments A and B. If the syntax

CALL EXTRACT IN(A) OUT(B)

were allowed, the readability of the program would be improved. Also, the compiler could do more to enforce the usage of data. For instance, the compiler could prevent EXTRACT from changing A, if A were defined as "read-only" to module EXTRACT.

When data coupling is used, parameter lists sometimes tend to get large. The PL/I language provides a useful way to document the parameters of a module, as shown below:

DECLARE TRIP ENTRY (CHAR(*) VAR, CHAR(4), FIXED);
CALL TRIP (A,B,C);

The DECLARE statement documents the fact that TRIP expects three parameters. The first parameter is a variable-length character string, the second is a four-byte character string, and the third is a fixed-point number.

In addition to being a useful means of documenting interfaces, the compiler uses this information to verify the interface at execution time. If the actual arguments don't match the specification in the DECLARE statement, the arguments will be converted to the proper form (for example, padding a character string with blanks). If the conversion can't be done, an error will be indicated—one example would be if A were a pointer.

A programming convention can be established to utilize this feature. In PL/I terms, whenever a module is created, a model DECLARE ENTRY statement should be created and placed in a compile-time library. The library member has a name related to the module name based on some convention. For instance, for module TRIP the corresponding library member could be named XTRIP. Whenever a programmer wishes to call a module from another module, he places an INCLUDE statement in his calling module, specifying X concatenated with the module name, such as:

%INCLUDE XTRIP;

When he compiles his module, the compiler replaces the INCLUDE statement with the corresponding DECLARE ENTRY statement.

Any use of the INCLUDE statement to insert data declarations into a module usually implies common or stamp coupling. This particular use of INCLUDE is not common or stamp coupling, since the DECLARE ENTRY does not define data to be shared by more than one module; it simply specifies the ordering and attributes of the parameters.

In addition to being a looser form of coupling, data coupling tends to reduce the scope of the coupling. If a program has only data coupling, each module is directly coupled only to the modules that it calls and to the modules that call it. If stamp or common coupling is present, all modules referencing the data structure, even if they reference different parts of it, are coupled to one another. Therefore data coupling reduces the number of modules that are coupled as well as the magnitude of the coupling.

Note that external coupling has a similar effect when compared to common coupling.

The matter of indirect coupling (A is coupled to B, B is coupled to C, hence there is some relationship between A and C) is discussed in Chapter 10.

CONTROL VERSÚS DATA COUPLING

In most cases it is easy to distinguish between control coupling and data coupling by examining the parameters passed. However, for certain types of parameters it is more difficult to distinguish between control information and data information. There are two guidelines that may assist here. First, the classification of the parameters (control and data) is dependent upon how the sending module perceives them, not how the receiving module perceives them. In Figure 4.13, if A passes x to B and A perceives x as data, then A and B are data coupled, even if B executes differently based on the value of x. If A perceives x as control information (i.e., A is telling B what to do), then A and B are control coupled.

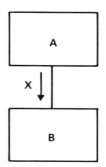

FIGURE 4.13.   Control versus data coupling

The same discussion applies to information returned from a module, such as return codes or error flags. If B passes a return code back to A, saying "I've failed in performing my function" (implying that A can do whatever it wants), then this return code is *data.* If B passes a return code saying "I've failed; write error message XYZ," then A and B are control coupled because B is telling A what to do.

A second point is that control information is usually artificially created (over and above what is being processed by the program). For instance, suppose the function of B is to process a command. If A simply passes a command to B and B examines the command to determine how to process it, then A and B are data coupled. If A passes a command to B and, in addition, passes a code saying "process this XYZ command," then A and B are control coupled.

This second point also illustrates another disadvantage of control coupling. Control information is artificially created within the program and is extraneous. Hence control information increases the complexity of the program because the program is dealing with extraneous and unnecessary data.

PASSING POINTERS OR ADDRESSES

In some programming languages it is possible to pass the pointer or address of data as an explicit parameter. For instance, this can be done in PL/I by passing POINTER variables.

When analyzing coupling in a situation where pointers or addresses are present, do not base your analysis on the pointers; base it on what the pointers eventually point to. For example, P is a pointer pointing to data structure S. Module A calls module B passing P as a parameter. Modules A and B are not data coupled; they are stamp coupled.

Direct reference between the modules	Y		N	N	N	N	N
Modules are packaged together		Y	N	N	N	N	N
Some interface data is external or global			Y	Y	N	N	N
Some interface data is control information					Y	N	N
Some interface data is in a data structure			Y	N		Y	N
Content coupling	X	X					
Common coupling			X				
External coupling				X			
Control coupling					X		
Stamp coupling						X	
Data coupling							X

FIGURE 4.14.   Determining coupling

In Chapter 3 it was pointed out that a module could meet the definitions of several types of strengths. When this occurs, the module is defined to have the highest strength of the types for which it meets the definition. The same situation often occurs with coupling, and the convention is the same. If modules A and B appear to be common coupled and data coupled, then they are defined to be common coupled (the higher of the two). However, note that high strength and low coupling is the goal.

The reasons for this lie in the definitions of strength and coupling. Strength is a measure of the relationships between the elements in a module. Since the values of strength are supersets and subsets of one another, a module's strength is the highest relationship that exists among the elements. Coupling is a measure of the relationships among modules. The coupling between two modules is the tightest relationship between those two modules, the highest degree of coupling that those two modules exhibit.

The decision table in Figure 4.14 will assist in determining the coupling between any pair of modules. Blanks in the top half of the table indicate "don't care" conditions.

Table 4.1 summarizes the attributes of each type of coupling.

Table 4.1   Coupling Attributes

Coupling	Independence from Other Modules	Suscepti- bility to Errors	Usability in Other Programs	Extensibility
Data	High	Low	High	High
Stamp *	Medium	Medium	Medium	Medium
Control	Medium	Medium	Medium	Medium
External	Low to medium	High	Low to medium	Low
Common *	Low	High	Low	Low
Content	Low	High	Low	Low

* Varies based on the extent of common and/or stamp coupling. Extensive use of common and/or stamp coupling in a large program further degrades the attributes.

CHAPTER 5

OTHER MEASURES

Although module strength and coupling are the major measures of modularity (module independence), there is a second set of measures and guidelines that plays an important role in program design. The following guidelines have an effect on the modularity of a program or system: simplicity, module size, recursion, predictable modules, initialization, decision structure, data access, restrictive modules, input/output isolation, internal subroutines. They are used to guide the designer during the design process and also to improve a first-pass program design.

SIMPLICITY

Simplicity is an extremely important design objective. Everything else being equal, the simplest solution, design, or interface is the best. This statement is easy to remember and almost intuitively obvious, yet it is often forgotten. Assume, everything else being equal, that there are two possible solutions, a simpler one and a more complex one. The simpler one, being easier to understand, has a more positive effect on the future maintenance and modification costs of the program.

An idea related to simplicity is that of minimum commitment, wherein the solution of a problem is restricted to solving no more than the immediate problem at hand. A program, module, interface, or other element should not be designed to do more than it is required to do. A module can be generalized where it makes sense to allow it to be used in various contexts, but overgeneralizations should be avoided. It makes sense to generalize a square root module to operate on both integer and floating-point input, but it doesn't make sense to generalize the module to perform cube roots. A reasonable guideline is to allow flexibility of data but to avoid excessive flexibility of function.

Many people have some unfounded ideas about designing a generalized program. They feel that generality has to be achieved via open-ended and extendible modules and interfaces, usually with extensive common areas or control block structures. In most cases program designs of this type display low strength and high coupling.

A program can be designed to satisfy all possible predicted uses for the next 20 years, or it can be designed as a simple solution to the immediate problem at hand. The former situation should be avoided because we have shown that we are poor prophets concerning the future modifications of a program. Also, such programs tend to be difficult to change. The most successful programs are those that start out by providing a simple solution to the immediate problem. Such programs tend to be easier to extend.

MODULE SIZE

Module size is another measure of modularity because it is related to module independence. A 2,000-statement program consisting of 30 modules must have a greater degree of internal independence than an equivalent program of only one module, even if the 30 modules have high coupling and low strength. The mere subdivision of a program into pieces that are separately compiled enforces a certain degree of independence, since it is more difficult to intertwine two pieces of code if they are in modules that are separately compiled.

In addition to its contribution to independence module size is related to clarity, or understandability. If a module's interfaces and function are well defined, the remaining item that a programmer who is designing and coding the module must grasp is its logic. The smaller the module, the easier the job is of understanding the logic of a module. Various studies have suggested that a module's size should be small enough so that its program statements fit on a single sheet of paper.[20]

Module size also has a bearing on the ease with which a program can be tested. Consider a module that has a two-way branch, followed by a three-way branch, then a four-way branch, and then a two-way branch. In other words, the module does one of two things, then one of three things, then one of four things, and lastly one of two things. If these decisions are independent, then the module has 48 unique paths ($2 \times 3 \times 4 \times 2$). To test all paths, 48 tests are required. If the module is designed as two modules, where the first module does one of two things, then one of three things, and the second module does one of four things, then one of two things, the number of tests is only 14 (six for the first module and eight for the second module). If loops were present in the module, the difference would be even larger. Thus smaller modules provide more test points, with a resultant reduction in the total number of tests.

To appreciate this problem even more, consider Figure 5.1, which represents a flow diagram of a simple module. Assuming all of the decisions are independent of one another (admittedly the worst case situation), the module contains 608,400 unique paths! This is obtained by squaring the sum of 5^4 plus 5^3 plus 5^2 plus 5. If this module could be split down the middle, the number of unique test paths is reduced to 1,560 (780 in each module), still a large number but significantly lower than 608,400.

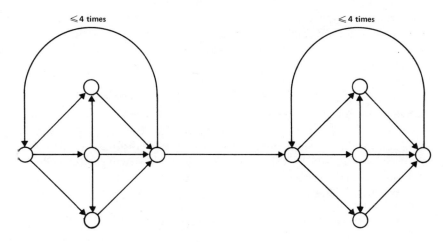

FIGURE 5.1. How many paths?

Module size is an important factor since it is related to a program's independence, understandability, and ease of testing. As a general guideline, modules should contain between 10 and 100 executable high-level source-language statements, with most modules containing between 40 and 60 statements.

This conclusion has been reached independently by others for a variety of reasons. Weinberg postulated that a module should have no more than 30 statements, based on the capacity of the human mind (30 statements is about all that a person can master at one time).[27] Mills suggests that a segment of code be small enough to fit on one page, primarily for readability.[20] Ferdinand, based on a theory of complexity, showed a relationship between module size and system size to minimize complexity.[12] For instance, he concluded that if the system size is 32,000 statements, the optimal module size is 40 statements. If the system size is 100,000 statements, the optimal module size is 60 statements.

RECURSION

Recursion occurs when a module is a subordinate of itself, that is, when a module calls itself or when it calls another module, which calls another module . . . which calls the original module.

Programmers usually steer clear of recursion because they do not fully understand it. Also, the module-linkage mechanisms of some operating systems and some programming languages do not allow recursive programming. Yet the use of recursion in a modular design should be encouraged. In certain situations it is the natural solution, and its use tends to simplify the program's logic. A simple example illustrates this.

Assume a module must be written whose function is "write error message to terminal user, or, if this is unsuccessful, notify system operator." There are two arguments passed to this module, the error message and a terminal number. Consider two alternate implementations of the module WRITEMSG. The first alternative is to write the statements that write the message to the terminal and then check for an error; if one occurs, write a message to the operator's terminal.

```
WRITEMSG: PROCEDURE (MSG,TNO)
              •
              •
              •
Set up and write msg to terminal
              •
              •
              •
```

```
        IF NO ERROR, RETURN
        ELSE
                    •

                    •

                    •
        Set up and write msg to operator's
            terminal
        RETURN
```

Some duplicate coding can be detected here, and one might decide, at the expense of added complexity, to share some of these statements between the "two halves" of WRITEMSG.

Another technique that could be used is recursion. If the message can't be written to the indicated terminal, the module calls itself, passing an error message and the operator's terminal number as arguments. The check to see if TNO equals SOTNO was added to prevent a loop in the event that an error occurs on the operator's terminal.

```
    WRITEMSG: PROCEDURE (MSG,TNO)
                    •

                    •

                    •
    set up and write msg to terminal
                    •

                    •

                    •
    IF NO ERROR OR TNO=SOTNO, RETURN
        ELSE CALL WRITEMSG (EMSG,SOTNO)
        RETURN
```

Although the example above is a valid use of recursion, it doesn't point out the real values of the technique. The first advantage of recursion is that it is the simplest and most natural way of expressing the solutions to certain problems. The second advantage is that it can eliminate the need for complex storage management, as shown in the following example.

Consider a module that deals with bills-of-material. A bill-of-material is a list of the parts that are immediately subordinate to another part. A part can be composite or atomic. A composite part is a named collection of subordinate parts, represented by a bill-of-material. An atomic part is a part with no subordinate parts. An example of a bill-of-material structure is shown in Figure 5.2. Part A (a particular type of car) is a composite part. Its bill-of-material would list parts B, C, and D. Parts A, B, C, D, E, and G are composite parts; parts F and H are atomic parts.

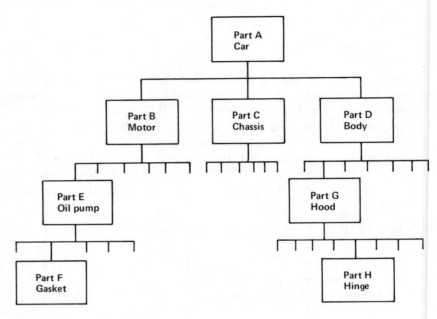

FIGURE 5.2.   Bill-of-material

The function of the program is to create a table of atomic parts making up any composite part. This is basically a tree-search problem, and recursion is a natural solution to this type of problem. Module BOM, shown in Figure 5.3, has three parameters—a part number, a table that will contain the atomic parts, and a count of the number of current entries in the table. Whenever module BOM is called, it will find the atomic parts making up the part indicated in the input parameters. FINDIMM is another module that, given a part number, returns a list and count of immediate subordinate parts. The logic of FINDIMM is not shown, but presumably it reads a bill-of-material from a data base.

PL/I defaults most variables to the AUTOMATIC storage class. Variables IMMSUB, N, and I have the AUTOMATIC storage class. An AUTOMATIC variable exists only within the current activation, or generation, of a module. When module BOM is executing, there can be multiple copies of IMMSUB, N, and I, one for each recursive

```
BOM: PROCEDURE (PART,TABLE,COUNT) RECURSIVE;
DCL PART FIXED BINARY (31),
     TABLE (*) FIXED BINARY (31),
     COUNT FIXED BINARY (15);
DCL IMMSUB (20) FIXED BINARY (15);
DCL (N,I) FIXED BINARY (15);
CALL FINDIMM (PART,IMMSUB,N);
IF N = 0 THEN DO;
             COUNT = COUNT + 1;
             TABLE (COUNT) = PART;
             END;
       ELSE DO I = 1 TO N;
             CALL BOM (IMMSUB(I),TABLE,COUNT);
             END;
END BOM;
```

FIGURE 5.3.   Module BOM

invocation of BOM. These copies can be viewed as entries in a push-down stack. The current copy is the one associated with the current invocation of BOM. When BOM returns to itself, the old current copy is discarded and the top entry on the stack becomes the new current copy.

This automatic management of storage makes the implementation of BOM fairly straightforward. Implementing BOM as a nonrecursive module would be more complicated, since the programmer of BOM would have to code his own management of the levels of IMMSUB, N, and I.

Recursion is the most natural method of solving certain problems, such as tree searching or following paths through a network. Although any recursive module can be coded as a nonrecursive module, recursion can simplify the logic of a module and also make more efficient use of storage (because storage is allocated on an as-needed basis).

PREDICTABLE MODULES

A predictable, or well-behaved, module is one that, when given the identical inputs, operates identically each time it is called.[22] A predictable module also operates independent of its environment.

The most common violation of the first statement occurs when a module keeps track of its own state. The best example of this is a module containing a statement like "IS THIS THE FIRST TIME I'VE BEEN ENTERED? IF YES, THEN. . . ." Modules of this sort are usually unusable in more than one place in a program, which violates one of the basic principles of composite design.

Consider a module called GET NEXT INPUT TRANSACTION. Assume that this module, on its first execution, requests the operator to mount the required tape. Later, when modifying the program, there is a need in another part of the program for this same function (but using a different tape on a different tape drive). Only one of the two tapes will get mounted, depending on who calls this module first! The only way out is by spending more money either by writing a new module or by making this module predictable.

A module that alters storage within itself (static storage) is also probably unpredictable. A module that can perform its function only if module XYZ has been previously executed is another example of an unpredictable module.

INITIALIZATION

Since an initialization module has classical strength, how and where initialization is performed is a valid question. To begin answering this, consider Figure 5.4, which represents part of a program structure. Because the program involves the reading of a transaction file, the file must be opened and closed. In the figure these processes are performed in an initialization module. There are three problems here:

1. If the characteristics of the transaction file are altered, modules READ TRANSACTION and INITIALIZATION will probably have to change. Since they are far removed from one another in the structure, one might easily be overlooked. Also, high module independence has not been achieved, since these two modules are closely related.
2. Module SUMMARIZE TODAY'S TRANSACTIONS is not easily used in another program or in a different context in this program because the file must be opened before the module is called and closed after it returns. In other words, the usage rules of this module are more complicated than need be.

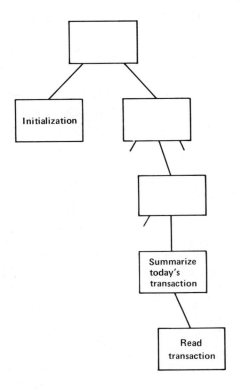

FIGURE 5.4. Initialization

3. Interfaces are more complicated than necessary because information on the opened file must be passed from INITIALIZATION all the way through the program to READ TRANSACTION.

The answer to the initialization question is simply to initialize (and clean up) within the module for which the initialization and termination is being done. To look at it another way, perform initialization and termination processing as far down in the structure as possible, but not to a depth that would create an unpredictable module. In the case of Figure 5.4 the opening and closing of the file should be done in the module SUMMARIZE TODAY'S TRANSACTIONS, so that its logic would look something like the following:

```
OPEN TFILE
DO UNTIL END-OF-FILE
    CALL READ TRANSACTION (TFILE,A)
    SUMMARIZE
END
CLOSE TFILE
RETURN
```

If the opening and closing were put down one level farther into module READ TRANSACTION, that module could become unpredictable.

DECISION STRUCTURE

Whenever possible, it is desirable to arrange modules and decisions in those modules in such a way that modules directly affected by a decision are subordinate (beneath) the module containing the decision. This is an attempt to hide the results of a decision in a module from the calling module. The decision-structure guideline also tends to keep decisions affecting program control at a high level in the program structure.

In Figure 5.5 module D contains a decision x. Decision x eventually determines whether or not module C will be executed. This situation does not adhere to the guideline because module C is directly affected by decision x, yet module C is not subordinate to module D.

What are the consequences of this? Module D has to pass the results of this decision back to B, possibly as a control switch (implying control coupling). Module B tests the switch to determine whether to continue executing or to return to A. Hence module B is, in a sense, repeating decision x. Module B then returns the switch to module A (again, possible control coupling). Module A then tests the switch to determine if C should be called (another duplication of decision x).

Violations of the decision-structure guideline lead to control coupling and redundant decisions in the program. The cure for these problems is to redesign the affected part of the structure, either by moving the decision element higher in the structure or by taking the modules affected by the decision and trying to place them subordinate to the module containing the decision. For instance, depending on the actual functions of the modules in Figure 5.5, it

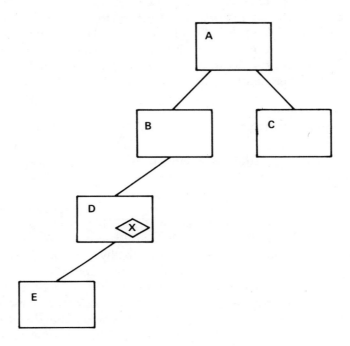

FIGURE 5.5. Decision structure

might be possible to have module D call module C directly (make C subordinate to D).

In practice it is not possible to correct all violations of the decision structure guideline without weakening the strengths of some of the modules in the program. Improvements in decision structure should be made only when they don't cause any module's strength to decrease. Also, "upward propagation" of such decision information as error indications or end-of-file switches is often unavoidable. However, try to minimize the number of exceptions to the guideline.

DATA ACCESS

Another useful objective is to minimize the amount of data that any module can reference. Chapter 4 pointed out that elimination of common, external, and stamp coupling is a big step in achieving this objective. The data passed to any module should be minimized to include only the specific data needed. Instead of passing an entire record or data structure to a module, pass only the individual fields needed. Try to isolate knowledge of any particular data structure or record format to a single module (or small number of modules), possibly by using informational-strength modules where multiple functions must be performed on one data structure.

RESTRICTIVE MODULES

A restrictive module is a module whose general use has been needlessly restricted, either in its documentation or code. The use of restrictive modules should be avoided.

In the development of an operating system a module was defined whose function was "convert JCL to JCLS." JCL was a sequence of 80-byte records, and JCLS was a chained list of these 80-byte records. Hence the function of this module was really "convert a sequential stream of 80-byte records to a chain of 80-byte records."

This is a restrictive module. It could probably be used elsewhere, but its function description really describes one particular use of the module, not its real function. The fact that it is misnamed will hinder its being discovered for other uses. Also, using it in this misnamed fashion in another context will be confusing. The problem could have been avoided simply by correctly documenting the function of the module.

In addition to the documentation being inaccurate, the code in this module is also unnecessarily restrictive. The fact that this particular use of the module involved 80-byte records caused the programmer to wire the value 80 into his code. The module's potential use in the future or in other contexts could have been improved by accepting the record length as an input parameter.

A second example of a restrictive module is a module that makes assumptions about its environment or, in particular, about its caller. As an example, a module was written to accept a string of messages as input, format them, and write them to a terminal. At first glance this module appeared to be useful in several parts of the program. However, this assumption proved to be false because of the implementation of the module. The programmer writing the module assumed that it would be called by only one other module. Therefore, before writing the string of messages, this module wrote an additional message: "ERROR IN FUNCTION XYZ. ERROR MESSAGES FOLLOW." Fortunately, this has a happy ending: The mistake was discovered and the extra message was removed. In this case the calling module inserted this message into the string before calling the message module.

It is possible to go overboard by viewing almost any module as restrictive in some sense and then attempting to cure it. Such a process will contradict the goals of simplicity discussed earlier in this chapter. Remember that a restrictive module is one whose function is actually broader than it is documented to be, or one that could be more flexible by changing wired-in values to input parameters, or one that makes assumptions about its caller. Correcting a restrictive module in one of these categories does not contradict the ideas of simplicity.

INPUT/OUTPUT ISOLATION

Isolating a program's input/ouput operations into a small number of modules is a desirable goal. For instance, all of the primitive functions performed for a particular file could be isolated into an informational-strength module.

This strategy enhances the portability and extensibility of a program. The program can be converted to a different computing system or operating system more easily if the system-dependent functions are isolated in a small number of places. The program could be converted from a sequential file environment to a data base environment by simply unplugging these input/output modules and plugging in a new set reflecting the new environment.

INTERNAL SUBROUTINES

An internal subroutine or procedure is a called piece of code that physically resides in the calling module. In terms of composite design an internal subroutine is not a module, although it has many of the characteristics of a module. Internal procedures should be avoided for the following reasons:

1. It is difficult to isolate an internal procedure for testing (unit testing).
2. It is difficult to call an internal procedure from modules other than the one that it is physically imbedded in.
3. Unless a great deal of discipline is used during the coding of

modules containing internal procedures, the internal procedures may have poor degrees of coupling to their calling procedure.

Some of these disadvantages can be eliminated, for instance, in PL/I, by using the INCLUDE facility to copy the internal procedure into the module during its compilation. However, this may result in having physical copies of the internal procedure in more than one module, which means that modification of the procedure requires recompilation of all the modules containing it.

In general, if an internal procedure seems justified, don't do it; make it a module.

CHAPTER 6

COMPOSITE ANALYSIS

The previous chapters discussed the what and the why of composite design. Armed with this information, one could be relatively successful in leaving this book and designing a program. However, the flow of composite design has not yet really been discussed. This chapter covers the process of actually producing the structural design of a program. Chapter 7 contains some additional examples.

The structural-design process follows the external-design process (specifying the external characteristics of the program or system) and precedes the module design processes (precisely defining the interface and logic of each module). There are three steps in the structural design process:

1. Starting with the problem statement (or functional or external specification), design the structure of the entire program or system using one or more forms of analysis. Note that when designing a system (a collection of related programs), an intermediate step is usually necessary. Before the system can be decomposed into modules, it must be decomposed into independent programs, or components. (This is discussed in more detail in Chapter 8.)
2. Review the completed structural design, trying to maximize module strength and to minimize coupling.
3. Review the design again, using the guidelines of Chapter 5 (decision structure, input/output isolation, restrictive modules,

data access, size, recursion, predictable behavior) and the review process described in Chapter 8.

Note that this is an iterative process. Several passes through these steps are often necessary to optimize the structure. Also, discoveries made during later processes often require at least a partial revision of the structure. For instance, errors in the structure may be uncovered during the module logic design process.

The design process, by definition, is a creative activity. Composite analysis, a technique for designing modular programs, does not replace creativity; it is meant to channel creativity in the right direction.

Composite analysis is a top-down reasoning process. It involves iterating between defining sections of the program structure to supply functions and then generating new functional requirements from the completed sections of the structure. Composite analysis is also a rough formalization of the design process. In this form it will probably not strictly apply to any single design. The designer will have to adapt it, massage it, and compromise it to fit the particular problem he is trying to solve. In addition, two people independently designing the same program using composite analysis will probably arrive at two different, but probably equally good, modular structures.

The basis of composite analysis is that the structure of the program should resemble the structure of the problem. To accomplish this, composite analysis involves an analysis of the problem structure and, in particular, the flow of data through the problem and the transformations that occur on that data. The rationale behind this is that problem structures are almost always defined in purely functional terms. Consequently one way to arrive at a program structure with a functional organization (high module strength) is to model it after the problem structure.

Note that in the preceding paragraph the word *structure* is stressed. Composite analysis is totally based on structure. When using it, do not think in terms of procedure, time, sequence, or which event has to happen first. Think about what the program has to do; do not think about when the program has to do something.

The principal steps of composite analysis are:

1. Identify the problem structure.
2. Identify the principal input and output data streams in the problem.
3. Identify the points in the problem structure where these data streams begin and end.

4. Decompose this problem into a set of subordinate modules.
5. Repeat the process, viewing each module from step 4 as a new subproblem.

This chapter describes the steps of composite analysis, defines some additional guidelines, and then illustrates their use in an example. The next chapter will illustrate other examples.

PROBLEM STRUCTURE (STEP 1)

The first step is sketching out a rough picture of the problem. This sketch should be in functional, not procedural, terms. Most, if not all, problems can be represented by a linear chain of three to ten processes. The chain represents data flow within the problem, not necessarily the execution flow of the processes.

As an example, consider a simple airlines reservation system. It is driven by input from remote terminals. The major types of input are requests for information (seats available, flights), sales of tickets, and passenger check-in's. The rough structure of this problem is shown in Figure 6.1.

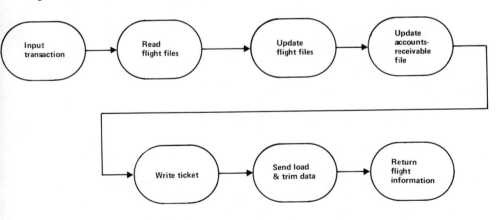

FIGURE 6.1. Problem structure

Note that this diagram is nonprocedural. For instance, on a request for seating information only a few of the steps are performed. Also, for a ticket sale we are not concerned about whether the ticket is written before or after the flight file is updated.

EXTERNAL DATA STREAMS (STEP 2)

Identify the streams of data that are both external and conceptual. An external stream of data is one that begins and/or ends outside of the system. A conceptual stream of data is a stream of related data that is independent of any physical input-ouput device. For instance, several conceptual streams may be coming from one input device or one stream may be coming from several input devices.

A good example here is OS/360. The input reader program may be reading from a physical input device (for example, a card reader). However, there are two conceptual streams here, the JCL statements and the SYSIN (those records following a DD * or DD DATA JCL statement). Since several input devices can be active simultaneously, the JCL stream is coming from several sources.

In the airlines reservation system the external conceptual streams are the input transactions, tickets, flight information, and load and trim data.

POINTS OF HIGHEST ABSTRACTION (STEP 3)

Most problems have one major input stream (the primary source of input) and one major output stream (the primary result). From the streams identified in step 2, identify the major external conceptual streams of data (both input and output) in the problem. Then, using the diagram of the problem structure, determine the points of highest abstraction for these streams.

If data flow is traced through the problem structure as shown in Figure 6.2, the major data streams are seen to pass through the problem structure, changing form as they do so. Tracing the input stream, one normally finds that the input stream becomes more and more abstract as it moves through the problem. Eventually a point is hit in the problem structure where the input stream seems to disappear. This point is identified as the point of highest abstraction for the input stream.

Similarly, the output stream can be traced back into the problem. As it is traced back, the output stream undergoes certain transformations and becomes more abstract. Eventually a point is hit where the most abstract form of the output first exists. This is the point of highest abstraction for the output stream.

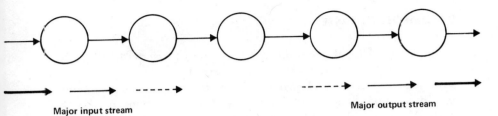

Major input stream   Major output stream

FIGURE 6.2.   Changes in abstraction

Each problem is assumed to have major input and output streams of data. Any stream of data usually exists in many forms throughout the problem. For instance, in the airlines reservation system the input transaction can exist as spoken words (from customer to clerk), a request typed into terminal, a request received in digital form by computer, a request recorded on audit trail, a request parsed into its parts, or a request stored in an internal table.

The point of highest abstraction for a stream of data is the point in the problem structure where that data is farthest removed from its physical input or output form yet is still recognizable as being that particular stream of data. Hence in the airlines reservation system the most abstract form of the input transaction stream might be a validity-checked input transaction stored in an internal table.

The points of highest abstraction are determined for the major input and output streams. This defines two points on the problem structure. All information in the problem structure between these two points is called the *central transform* of the problem, as illustrated in Figure 6.3.

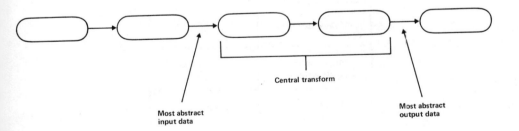

Central transform

Most abstract
input data

Most abstract
output data

FIGURE 6.3.   Points of highest abstraction

DECOMPOSITION (STEP 4)

The problem has now been broken into three parts. Take each of these parts and describe it as a function. Then the program structure is started as shown in Figure 6.4, where the functions of the three subordinate modules represent the functions of the three parts of the problem. The arguments passed are dependent on the actual problem, but the general pattern is shown in Figure 6.4.

The function of each module should be described in a short, concise, and specific phrase. Remember that the function of a module

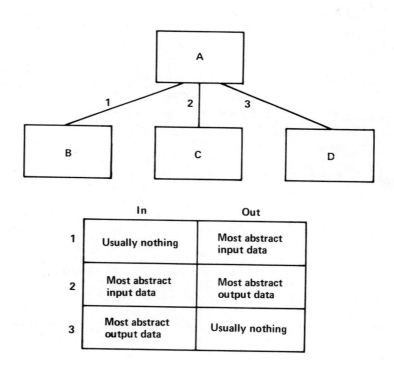

FIGURE 6.4. Starting the program structure

is a description of the transformations that occur when that module is called. It does not necessarily describe the processing contained wholly within that particular module. With composite analysis our objective is to define modules that have functional strength. In order to review some of the do's and don't's, it would be worthwhile to reread Chapter 3, on module strength.

When module A is called, the program or system executes. Hence the function of module A is equivalent to the function of the program. If the problem is "write a FORTRAN compiler," then the function of module A is "compile FORTRAN program."

Figure 6.4 shows that module B's output is the most abstract input data. Hence module B should be defined as a functional-strength module whose function involves obtaining the major stream of data. An example of a typical module B is "get next valid source statement in Polish form." Because module B's function involves obtaining data, it is referred to as a *source*-type module.

Module C represents the central transform of the program. Its purpose is to transform the major input stream into the major output stream. Its function should be a nonprocedural description of this transformation. Examples of typical module C's are "convert Polish form statement to machine language statement" or "using keyword list, search abstract file for matching abstracts." Any module whose function involves converting data from one form to another is called a *transform*-type module.

Module D's purpose is disposing of the major output stream. Module D, like the others, should be a functional-strength module. Module D's function is a description of the processing of the output stream. Examples of typical module D's are "produce daily activity report" or "display results of simulation." A module of this type is called a *sink*-type module.

RECURSING (STEP 5)

Now that the subordinates of module A have been defined (which are modules B, C, and D), the rest of the process involves defining the subordinates of these subordinates, and so on. This is done by picking one of these modules, viewing it as a subproblem, and starting again at step 1, defining the problem structure of this subproblem. In this analysis more than one major conceptual stream may be encountered in a particular subproblem. Hence, at this level it is possible to have several source or sink modules.

To analyze a module, temporarily view that module as an independent problem to solve. Some guidelines to follow in doing this follow:

1. The order in which individual modules are analyzed is not important. For instance, after completing step 4, we can start with B, C, or D.

2. It is not necessary to analyze one part of the structure completely before analyzing another part. For instance, after step 4 we don't have to analyze B, its subordinates, its subordinates' subordinates, and so on before starting to analyze C. In practice one usually jumps around the structure in the analysis.

3. Before a module's subordinate can be analyzed, that module must be completely analyzed. Thus, before analyzing a subordinate module of module XYZ, all of the immediate subordinates of module XYZ must be defined.

4. When decomposing a module into its subordinates, constantly review the entire structure for modules identical to the subordinates. Doing this makes possible the sharing of modules among different parts of the structure. If identical modules cannot be found but almost identical modules (with, say, identical function and similar interfaces, or with similar function) can be found, modify the modules to take advantage of higher fan-in to a common module.

5. When analyzing a subproblem, the source–transform–sink breakdown is more complex. The reason is that the major conceptual data stream of the subproblem normally enters or leaves through the module being analyzed. For instance, if a source-type module is being analyzed, the conceptual stream in this subproblem usually exits via this module when it returns to its caller, as shown in Figure 6.5. Hence this source-type module may actually appear to be a sink-type module with respect to this subproblem. The same applies to the analysis of a sink-type module. A transform-type module may act as both the source *and* sink with respect to its own subproblem.

This leads to the following three guidelines:

6. The subordinates of a source-type module are usually one or more source-type modules and a transform-type module. Occa-

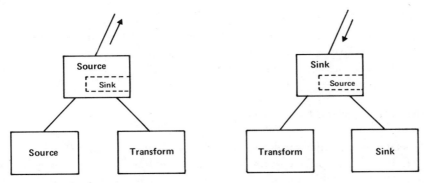

FIGURE 6.5. Decomposing source and sink modules

sionally a source-type module will have a sink-type module as a subordinate (for instance, to write out an error message).

7. The subordinates of a sink-type module are usually one or more sink-type modules and a transform-type module. Only rarely does a sink-type module have a source-type module as a subordinate (for instance, to obtain the format description of a report).

8. The subordinates of a transform-type module are usually transform-type modules. Some transform-type modules will also have sink- and/or source-type modules as subordinates.

STOPPING

Composite analysis is an iterative process, but obviously the process must eventually terminate. There are no explicit criteria for stopping the process, but the following guidelines can be used:

1. When none of the modules can be decomposed further into independent functional subordinate modules, then the process is complete. For instance, if the only apparent decomposition of a module leads to a set of modules having undesirable strength and coupling attributes, then this module should not be decomposed.

2. If you can completely visualize in your head the logic of a module (which normally indicates that the module has less than 50 statements), then decomposition of the module is probably unnecessary.

3. If the decomposition of a particular module leads to a set of small and extremely specialized modules whose use in other contexts or programs is unlikely, then decomposition of the module may be unnecessary.

PATIENT-MONITORING PROGRAM

To better understand the use of composite analysis, it will be used in an example. Assume a program must be designed to solve the following problem:

Design a patient-monitoring program for a hospital. Each patient is monitored by an analog device that measures such factors as pulse, temperature, blood pressure, and skin resistance. The program should read these factors on a periodic basis (specified for each patient). The program stores these factors in a data base. Safe ranges for each patient for each factor are specified (for example, patient X's valid temperature range is 98 to 99.5 degrees). If a factor falls outside of a patient's safe range, or if an analog device fails, the nurse's station is notified.

In a real-life case the problem statement would contain much more detail. However, this one is of sufficient detail to allow us to design the structure of the program. The first step is to outline the structure of the problem. This is shown in Figure 6.6. In the second step the external conceptual streams of data are identified. In this case two streams are present, factors from the analog device and warnings to the nurse. These represent the major input and output streams.

The point of highest abstraction of the input stream is the point

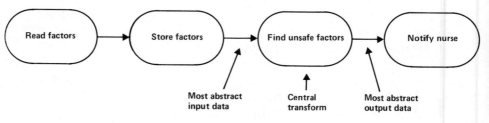

FIGURE 6.6.   Problem structure

at which a patient's factors are in a form where they can be compared with a list of critical ranges. The point of highest abstraction of the output stream is a list of unsafe factors (if any), as shown in Figure 6.6.

Design of the program's structure can now begin. The initial "top" modules of the program are illustrated in Figure 6.7.

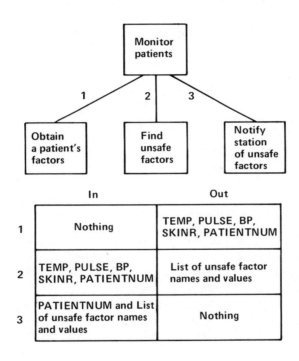

	In	Out
1	Nothing	TEMP, PULSE, BP, SKINR, PATIENTNUM
2	TEMP, PULSE, BP, SKINR, PATIENTNUM	List of unsafe factor names and values
3	PATIENTNUM and List of unsafe factor names and values	Nothing

FIGURE 6.7. The "top"

Module OBTAIN A PATIENT'S FACTORS will now be analyzed. From the problem statement one can deduce that this function (subproblem) has three parts:

1. Determine which patient to monitor next (based on their specified periodic intervals)
2. Read the analog device
3. Record the factors in the data base

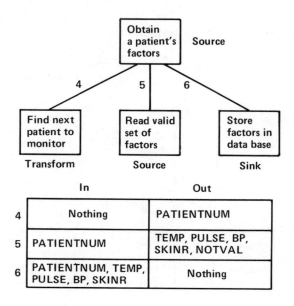

FIGURE 6.8. Decomposing OBTAIN

This leads to Figure 6.8. Module FIND NEXT PATIENT TO MONITOR represents some "choosing" algorithm to determine which patient is next. Note that transform-, source-, and sink-type modules have been created. NOTVAL is an output argument that is set if a valid set of factors wasn't available (for instance, if the particular analog device is inoperable).

Further analysis of READ VALID SET OF FACTORS and its subordinates yields the substructure in Figure 6.9. The diamond (decision) symbol indicates that the module NOTIFY STATION OF BAD TERMINAL is conditionally executed. That is, the nurses' station is notified only if the read from the analog device was unsuccessful.

Moving to another part of the structure, module FIND UNSAFE FACTORS is analyzed to arrive at the substructure in Figure 6.10. This subproblem has a simple structure, obtaining the safe ranges for a particular patient from a data base and then checking to see if one or more of the current measured values fall outside of these ranges. The last part of the structure is analyzed, yielding Figure 6.11.

The following sets of data are required in the program. These

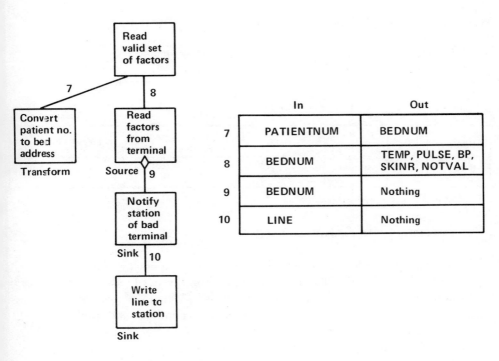

FIGURE 6.9.   Decomposing READ

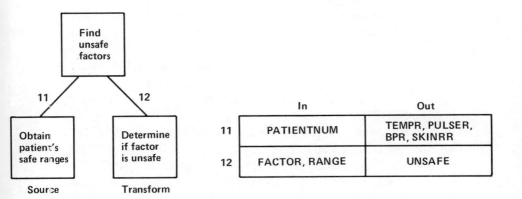

FIGURE 6.10.   Decomposing FIND

81

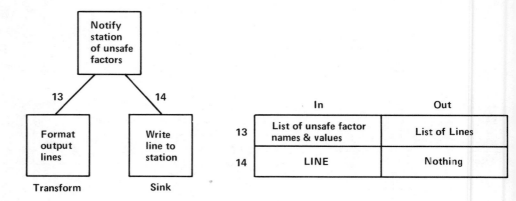

	In	Out
13	List of unsafe factor names & values	List of Lines
14	LINE	Nothing

FIGURE 6.11. Decomposing NOTIFY

sets of data could either be passed down as parameters from module MONITOR PATIENTS or else be read from files: (1) list of patient numbers and their monitor time intervals; (2) map of patient numbers to bed numbers; (3) list of patient numbers and their safe ranges.

The composite analysis of this program is now complete. However, the program has one decision-structure problem that will be corrected.

In Figure 6.12 note that module READ FACTORS FROM TERMINAL contains a decision asking "was the read from the terminal successful?" If the read wasn't successful, the nurse's station must be notified and the next patient to process must be found.

Modules directly affected by this decision are marked with an X. Note that these modules are not subordinate to READ FACTORS FROM TERMINAL. To correct this problem, two steps will be taken. First, the decision will be moved up to READ VALID SET OF FACTORS. This is done by merging READ FACTORS FROM TERMINAL into its calling module. FIND NEXT PATIENT TO MONITOR is now made a subordinate of READ VALID SET OF FACTORS. The function of READ VALID SET OF FACTORS then becomes READ NEXT PATIENT'S FACTORS. Figure 6.13 illustrates these corrections.

The completed structure of the patient-monitoring program is shown in Figure 6.14, and the interfaces are shown in Figure 6.15.

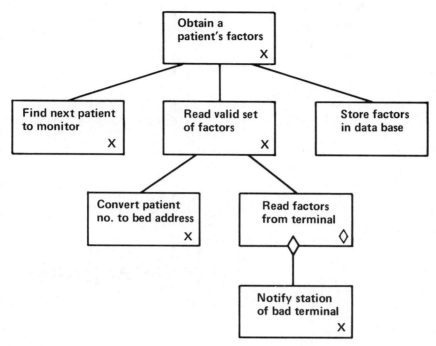

FıGURE 6.12.   Decision-structure problem

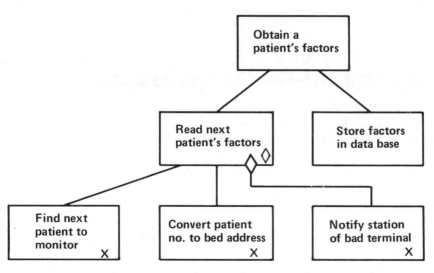

FıGURE 6.13.   Decision-structure problem corrected

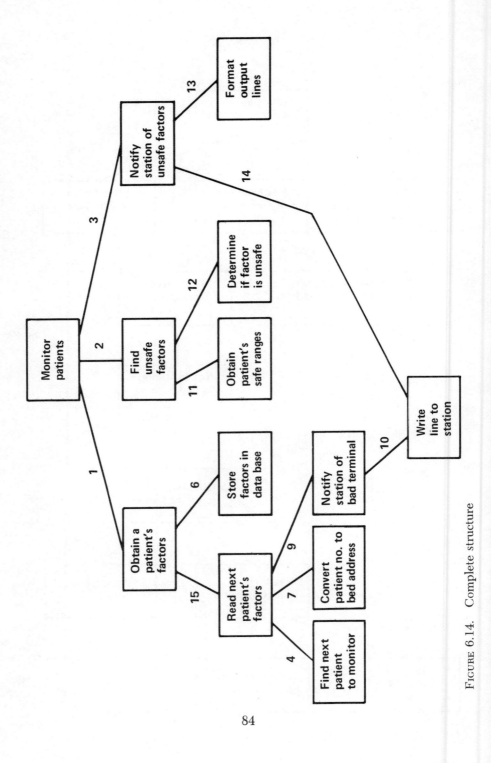

FIGURE 6.14. Complete structure

84

	In	Out
1	————————	TEMP, PULSE, BP, SKINR, PATIENTNUM
2	TEMP, PULSE, BP, SKINR, PATIENTNUM	List of unsafe factor names & values
3	PATIENTNUM & List of unsafe factor names & values	————————
4	————————	PATIENTNUM
6	PATIENTNUM, TEMP, PULSE, BP, SKINR	————————
7	PATIENTNUM	BEDNUM
9	BEDNUM	————————
10, 14	LINE	————————
11	PATIENTNUM	TEMPR, PULSER, BPR, SKINRR
12	FACTOR, RANGE	UNSAFE
13	List of unsafe factor names & values	List of lines
15	————————	TEMP, PULSE, BP, SKINR, PATIENTNUM

FIGURE 6.15. Interfaces

85

CHAPTER 7

DESIGN PROBLEMS

This chapter contains two design problems and their solutions. The first problem involves the modification of an existing program. The second problem is the design of an inventory-control program.

PROBLEM 1: PROGRAM MODIFICATION

The purpose of this problem is to examine the consequences of adding new functions to an existing program. The existing program is the patient-monitoring program in Figure 7.1. The problem is to determine where to add two additional functions, DISPLAY FACTORS ON PATIENT'S TERMINAL module and ADMINISTER ANTI-ARRYTHMIC DRUG module.

For the DISPLAY module the patient-monitoring program is to be modified so that after a patient's factors are read, they are immediately displayed on a graphics device attached to his terminal. The input to the module is the bed number and the four factors. The module returns no output. Note that output is data returned by a module. This module does have an *external effect*, the display on the terminal. (External effects are discussed further in Chapter 8.)

In the ADMINISTER module a device that is attached to the patient's terminal is immediately activated to stimulate his heart. This module should be invoked if a patient's blood pressure, pulse, and skin resistance simultaneously fall outside of the safe ranges. The input is the patient number and the quantity of drug. There is no output.

To solve this problem, experiment by considering the addition of the DISPLAY module to points A, B, and C and the ADMINISTER

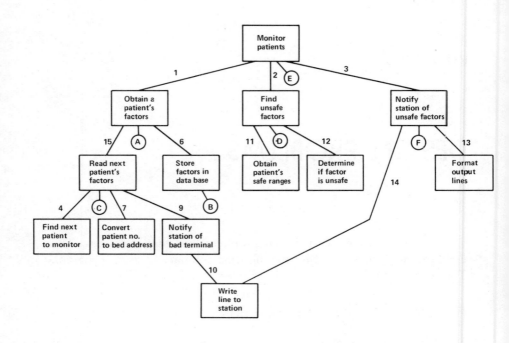

MODULE INTERFACES

	In	Out
1	————————————	TEMP, PULSE, BP, SKINR, PATIENTNUM
2	TEMP, PULSE, BP, SKINR, PATIENTNUM	List of unsafe factor names & values
3	PATIENTNUM & List of unsafe factor names & values	————————————
4	————————————	PATIENTNUM
6	PATIENTNUM, TEMP, PULSE, BP, SKINR	————————————
7	PATIENTNUM	BEDNUM
9	BEDNUM	————————————
10, 14	LINE	————————————
11	PATIENTNUM	TEMPR, PULSER, BPR, SKINRR
12	FACTOR, RANGE	UNSAFE
13	List of unsafe factor names & values	List of lines
15	————————————	TEMP, PULSE, BP, SKINR, PATIENTNUM

FIGURE 7.1.   Patient-monitoring program alternatives

88

module to points D, E, and F. For each alternative consider the following in determining the best alternatives:

1. Show all new and changed interfaces.
2. Describe the new function of every existing module where it has been changed.
3. Has the strength of any existing modules changed?
4. List all existing modules whose code has to be changed.

Evaluation of Alternatives

Alternative A. Interface 15 must change (BEDNUM must be returned as an output parameter so that it can be passed to the new module). No module functions or strengths change. Two modules have to change, READ NEXT PATIENT'S FACTORS to return BEDNUM as an output parameter and OBTAIN A PATIENT'S FACTORS to call the new module.

Alternative B. Interface 15 must change (BEDNUM must be an output) and interface 6 must change (BEDNUM is an input). Module STORE FACTORS IN DATA BASE changes in function to STORE FACTORS IN DATA BASE AND ON PATIENT'S TERMINAL. Its strength weakens to communicational. Three modules must be changed, READ NEXT PATIENT'S FACTORS, OBTAIN A PATIENT'S FACTORS, and STORE FACTORS IN DATA BASE.

Alternative C. No interfaces must change. Module READ NEXT PATIENT'S FACTORS changes in function to READ NEXT PATIENT'S FACTORS AND DISPLAY ON TERMINAL, which weakens its strength to communicational. Only one module must be changed.

Alternative B is clearly the poorest of the three. A and C are both reasonable choices. Although A involves a little more work, it is preferable since it preserves the high strength of all of the modules.

There are also three alternatives for the second module.

Alternative D. No interfaces must change. The function of module FIND UNSAFE FACTORS becomes FIND UNSAFE FACTORS AND ADMINISTER ANTI-ARRYTHMIC DRUG IF NECESSARY, and its strength weakens to communicational. Only one module has to be changed.

Alternative E. No interfaces must change. No module functions or strengths change. Only one module has to be changed.

Alternative F. No interfaces must change. The function of module NOTIFY STATION OF UNSAFE FACTORS changes to TAKE CORRECTIVE ACTION, but its strength doesn't change. One module has to be changed.

Alternative *D* is clearly the poorest of the three, with *E* and *F* being reasonable alternatives. *F* is slightly more desirable because new function should be placed as low as possible in the structure, providing that no module strengths are weakened. Of course, if module NOTIFY STATION OF UNSAFE FACTORS is being used in other programs, then *E* would be the proper choice. Figure 7.2 shows the new structure.

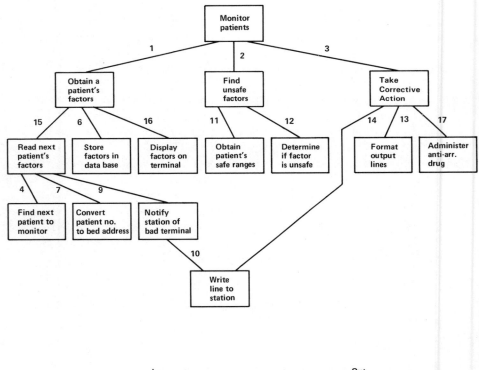

	In	Out
15	————————————	TEMP, PULSE, BP, SKINR, PATIENTNUM, BEDNUM
16	BEDNUM, TEMP, PULSE, BP, SKINR	————————————
17	PATIENTNUM, QUANTITY	————————————

FIGURE 7.2. New patient-monitoring program

PROBLEM 2: INVENTORY CONTROL

The inventory-control program in this problem must maintain a data base describing the parts in a warehouse and must process requests from remote terminals concerning that data base.

The warehouse has two categories of parts, atomic parts (a-parts) and composite parts (c-parts). The c-parts are simply named collections of a-parts. Seven commands can be entered from the terminals. The command names, operands, and brief descriptions of the commands are listed below.

1. DEFINE PART—partnumber, optional list of a-parts

   This command adds a part description to the data base. If the part is a c-part, then a list of its a-parts is given.

2. REDEFINE PART—partnumber, optional list of a-parts

   Same as DEFINE PART, but it overwrites an existing part description.

3. DELETE PART—partnumber

   Removes a part description (a-part or c-part) from the data base.

4. SET ORDER LIMIT—a-partnumber, number

   Defines a threshold for the part. If the number of parts in the inventory falls below the threshold, more parts are ordered. This command can be used to initially define or change the threshold.

5. QUERY PART—partnumber

   Display on the terminal all information associated with a part.

6. SHIP PARTS—partnumber, number, customer number

   If sufficient parts are available, the supply value in the data base is decremented and a ship notice is sent to the shipping department. If, in doing this, the quantity of parts falls below the order threshold, a notice is sent to the order department. If the command specifies a c-part, this process is iteratively carried out on the associated a-parts.

7. ADD PARTS—a-partnumber, number

   The supply value (on-hand amount) for this part is incremented by the specified amount.

Naturally each command has certain error conditions associated with it. For the sake of simplicity error conditions will be ignored, except that the need for error messages to be written to the terminals will be recognized.

Before designing the structure, it is reasonable to plan a tentative data base format. All parts will be represented as records in an indexed data set, where the part number is the key. The first two fields in the records are part number and type (a-part or c-part). If the part is an a-part, the remaining fields are order threshold, number on hand (supply), and list of c-parts containing this a-part. If the part is a c-part, the remaining field is a list of a-parts that make up this c-part.

The problem structure and the top of the program structure are shown in Figure 7.3. Note that at this level there is no central

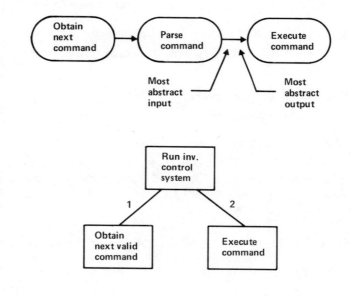

FIGURE 7.3.   Top of inventory-control system

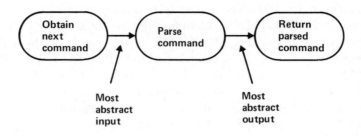

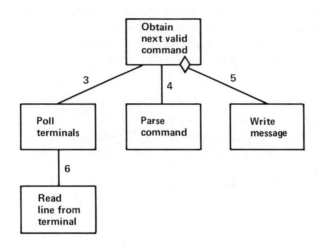

	In	Out
3	——	COMMAND, TERMADDR
4	COMMAND	COMMAND-TYPE, OPERANDS, ERROR-FLAG
5	TERMADDR, MESSAGE	——
6	TERMADDR	LINE

FIGURE 7.4. OBTAIN NEXT VALID COMMAND subproblem

93

transform. COMMAND-CODE is a number indicating the current command, TERMADDR identifies the terminal that the command was issued from, and FILENAME is the name of the data base. Decomposition of the source leg (OBTAIN NEXT VALID COMMAND) is straightforward and yields Figure 7.4. Module EXECUTE COMMAND will not be decomposed by composite analysis. The reason is that this point of the program is function-driven. EXECUTE COMMAND does not perform a static process on varying input (a data-driven module); it performs one of a class of processes that are selected based on the input. Hence EXECUTE COMMAND does not readily decompose into a source–transform–sink relationship. Instead it will be decomposed into seven subordinate functions, as shown in Figure 7.5. Each of these seven modules can now be analyzed. For instance, analysis of SHIP PART yields Figure 7.6.

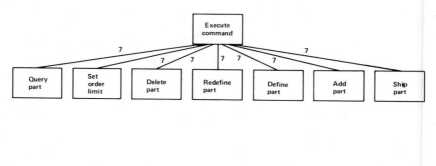

FIGURE 7.5. Decomposition of EXECUTE COMMAND

At this point several observations can be made:

1. There will be a number of modules that examine the data base records. Because this data base will probably be extended in the future, all functions directly processing data base records will be consolidated into one module (with informational strength). One exception will be made: QUERY will be allowed to examine the actual data base records because the QUERY command will always display all information about the part.

2. One command (REDEFINE) is actually a superset of two

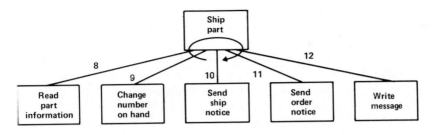

	In	Out
8	PART-NUMBER	TYPE, ON-HAND, THRESHOLD, LIST
9	PART-NUMBER, ON-HAND	ERRCODE
10	PART-NUMBER, NUMBER, CUSTOMER	———
11	PART-NUMBER, ON-HAND, THRESHOLD	———
12	TERMADDR, MESSAGE	———

FIGURE 7.6. Decomposition of SHIP PART

other commands, DELETE and DEFINE. Hence the REDE-
FINE module should use the DELETE and DEFINE modules.

3. TERMADDR (an identification of the terminal that issued the
command) was included in interfaces 1, 2, and 7 because
semantic errors (like a non-existent part number) may be
encountered during execution of the commands, which requires
error messages to be sent to the terminal. ERR was included
in interface 7 because of point 2 above.

Counter to what was implied in the previous figures, these points
weren't recognized initially in the design. For instance, in the
initial version of Figure 7.3, TERMADDR was not included in
interface 1. However, when the modules subordinate to EXE-
CUTE COMMAND were being analyzed, it became obvious that
TERMADDR was needed by these modules. At this time interfaces 1, 2, and 7 were updated to include TERMADDR. This
is a normal occurrence; it simply shows that program design
often resembles a feedback process.

4. An effort should be made to generalize the functions that process
the data base records so that the functions are usable in more
than one command.

The completed structure is shown in Figure 7.7. Descriptions of interfaces, although normally part of this diagram, were omitted for the sake of simplicity.

Because of the structure of this program, parallel processing (multitasking) could be easily added to this program to execute multiple commands simultaneously. Interface 2 could be changed to "start parallel task" instead of "call," and synchronization of the data base could be added. However, if external or common coupling were used (for instance, if TERMADDR was in a global data area), this change would be much more difficult.

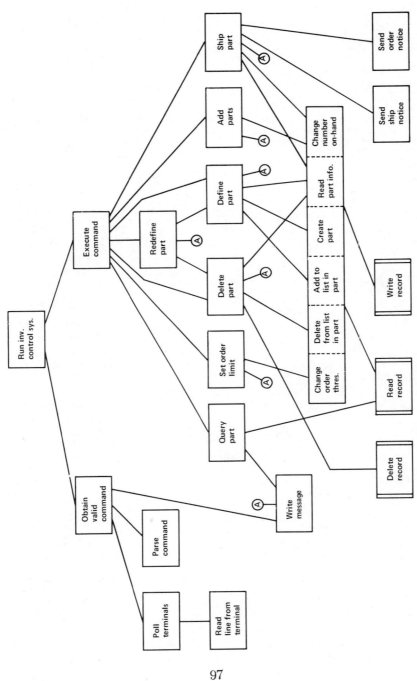

FIGURE 7.7. Inventory-control program

97

CHAPTER 8

MANAGEMENT OF DESIGN

This chapter is oriented to the project manager, project leader, chief programmer, and others who are in some way responsible for administering a programming project. A person functioning in one of these roles will be faced with some or all of the following questions:

1. How does composite design fit into the overall design process?
2. How does composite design relate to other programming techniques?
3. What are the advantages of composite design?
4. How will composite design help in management of the project?
5. What documentation should be produced?
6. Isn't composite design too rigid?
7. Doesn't composite design have a negative effect on execution speed?

This chapter will attempt to answer these and other questions.

One important consideration is the understanding of the meaning of guidelines, tradeoffs, and choices. Composite design is largely a collection of guidelines, not firm rules. Composite design doesn't imply that no program should ever have anything but functional strength and data coupling. What it does provide is a set of choices with an analysis of the ramifications of each alternative.

In the past a program might have contained common coupling because of an arbitrary choice by the designer or because he didn't consider any other alternatives. Composite design gives him a set of alternatives. He may still decide to use common coupling, but now hopefully because he did an objective analysis of the alternatives and decided to make a tradeoff based on a reason other than module independence.

Chapter 1 discussed certain benefits of composite design that result from its achieving high module independence. The resulting reduction in complexity has a positive effect on a program's quality, particularly in terms of reliability (number and significance of bugs), maintainability (cost of fixing a bug), and extensibility (cost of adding new function). Composite design also appears to have a positive effect on the cost of producing a program and the elapsed time of the project for the following reasons:

1. Programmer productivity during implementation and testing of the program appears to be higher than in normal programs. This is expected since productivity is inversely related to the complexity (interactions and dependencies) in a program. Composite design creates programs with independent parts, thus reducing the interactions and dependencies.

   Figure 8.1 describes the relationship between cost (in terms of cost per program statement) and system entropy (a measure of system size, structure, and complexity).[23] As composite design increases module independence, it reduces system entropy, thus increasing productivity.

   This relationship has been verified in a study of U.S. Air Force software.[19] The conclusion was that the cost per instruction in

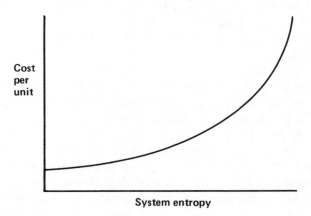

FIGURE 8.1.   Cost versus entropy

complex programs is inversely related to the degree of modularity of the programs. The use of the word *modularity* in the study meant dividing the program into many "functional modules," using a "formal parameter-passing technique," which seems to be consistent with the use of the word in this book.

2. Design changes are cheaper because they normally affect only a small subset of the program.
3. The design of the program is highly visible and more understandable. This increases productivity and also eases the process of communicating the design to the programmers who will implement the program and to any new programmers added to the project team.
4. Testing costs can be reduced. First, testing of the design is feasible (discussed later in this chapter). Second, because of high module independence and small module size, the complexity of module testing is reduced. Third, composite design leads to higher reliability, which lowers the testing and debugging costs.

Composite design decreases cost in another way, by simply focusing more attention on the design process. Figure 8.2 shows a trend noted by several authors, that the amount of effort expended on design influences the total cost of the project (for instance, see reference 24). From this, Figure 8.3 can be hypothesized, showing the relationship between total system cost and the fraction of that cost spent on design. This graph postulates that for any program there

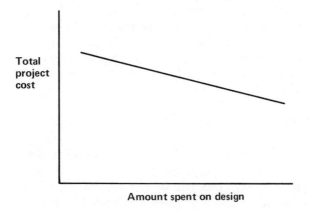

Amount spent on design

FIGURE 8.2.   Design cost versus total cost

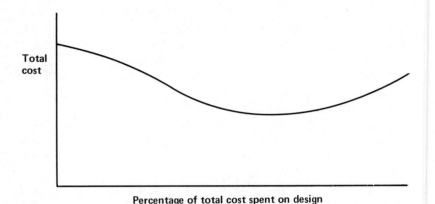

FIGURE 8.3.   Optimal design cost

is an optimal amount of money that should be spent on design. Spending less than this amount (which typifies most projects) increases the total cost. Spending too much money on design (a case that almost never occurs) probably also increases system cost, due to diminishing returns and the temptation to design an overly complex solution. Most programs fall on the left side of this curve. Composite design, by adding more rigor and attention to the design process, tends to move projects toward the center of the curve.

The Air Force study previously referenced shows a similar result. Three programming projects were examined in the study. Two of the programs had a considerable design effort, and the third had a small design effort. In the first two programs there was a lower ratio of errors per statement and most of the bugs were due to coding errors, which are usually much easier to diagnose and fix than design bugs. The third program had a larger ratio of errors per statement, and half of these bugs were due to design errors.

OVERALL DESIGN PROCESS

In order to relate composite design to the other design activities in a project, examine Figures 8.4 through 8.10, which illustrate the design steps for a large program or system. For a small- to moderate-sized program the steps in Figures 8.5 through 8.7 can be omitted. Composite design is the fifth step (Figure 8.8) in the process, the structural design of the system. Some aspects of composite design

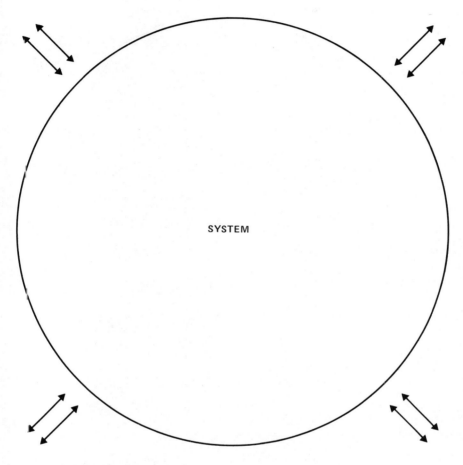

SYSTEM

PHASE: External design

ACTIVITY: Precise definition of the external characteristics of the system

METHODOLOGY: None known. The informal practices are experience in prior systems, systems analysis, and man-machine psychology. Also ingenuity, foresight, perception, etc.

OUTPUT: Precise description of the external characteristics (functions, inputs, outputs, human factors, reliability, performance) of the system

FIGURE 8.4. External design

103

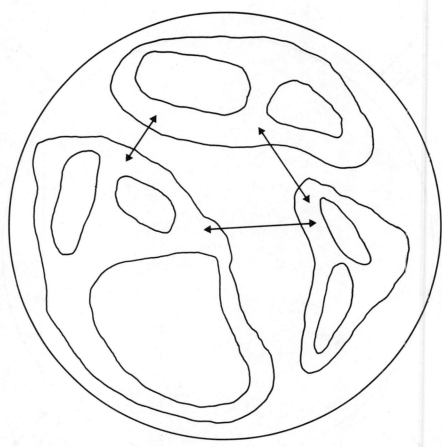

PHASE: System design

ACTIVITY: Definition of the internal architecture of the system

METHODOLOGY: None known. The system is usually subdivided into components
and subcomponents based on some criteria such as commonality
of function and/or data.

OUTPUT: Definitions of components and subcomponents and general descriptions of
component interfaces; descriptions of the component and subcomponent
organization in terms of control flow, data flow, task structure, and memory
structure.

FIGURE 8.5.   System architecture

104

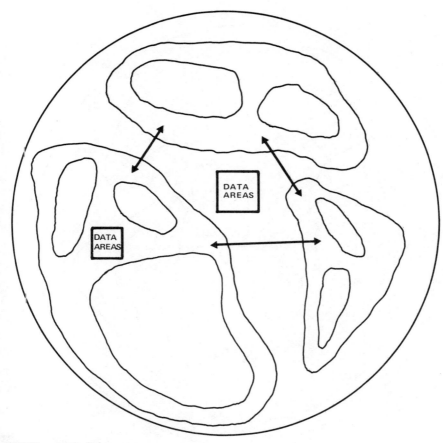

PHASE: Logic design

SUBPHASE: Component data design

ACTIVITY: Precise design of all component interfaces and all inter- and intracomponent
data areas (i.e., data global to the system and data global to a component)

METHODOLOGY: Composite design (use of coupling measures to minimize component
and subcomponent coupling); an interface language to describe interfaces
and data areas

OUTPUT: Precise description of component interfaces and inter- and intracomponent data areas

FIGURE 8.6.   Component data design

105

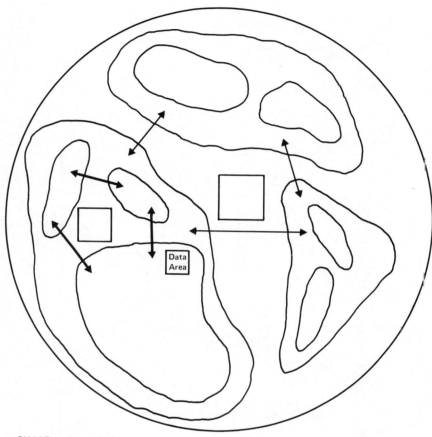

PHASE: Logic design

SUBPHASE: Subcomponent data design

ACTIVITY: Precise design of all subcomponent interfaces and all intrasubcomponent data areas

METHODOLOGY: Composite design (use of coupling measures to minimize coupling); an interface language to describe interfaces and data areas

OUTPUT: Precise description of subcomponent interfaces and intrasubcomponent data areas

FIGURE 8.7. Subcomponent data design

106

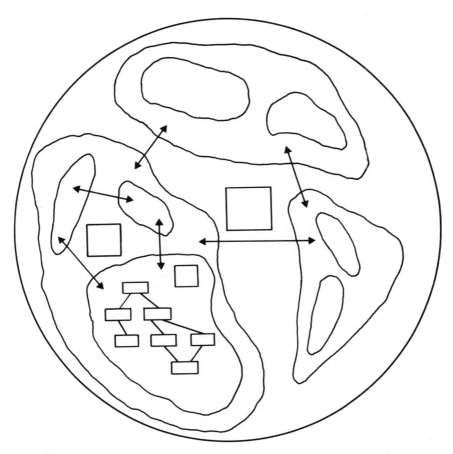

PHASE: Logic design

SUBPHASE: Structural design

ACTIVITY: Design the modular structure of each subcomponent

METHODOLOGY: Composite design

OUTPUT: Module structure diagrams of each subcomponent or component, showing all module interconnections, module functions, and general module interfaces

FIGURE 8.8. Structural design

107

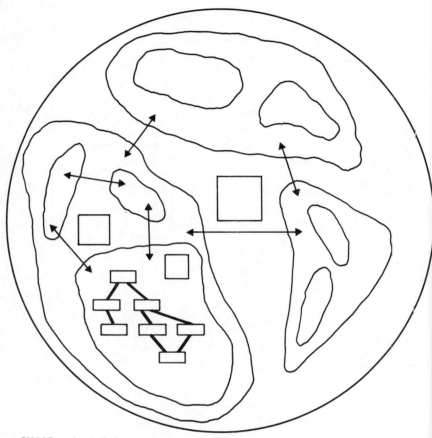

PHASE: Logic design

SUBPHASE: Module external design

ACTIVITY: For each module, precise definition of module name, function, inputs, outputs, and external effects

METHODOLOGY: An interface language

OUTPUT: An "external specification" for each module, containing the module's name, function, inputs, outputs, and external effects. This should constitute the first half of a module's "prologue"(commentary information preceding a module's source code statements). This information could also be placed in the input and output boxes in HIPO charts.

FIGURE 8.9. Module external design

108

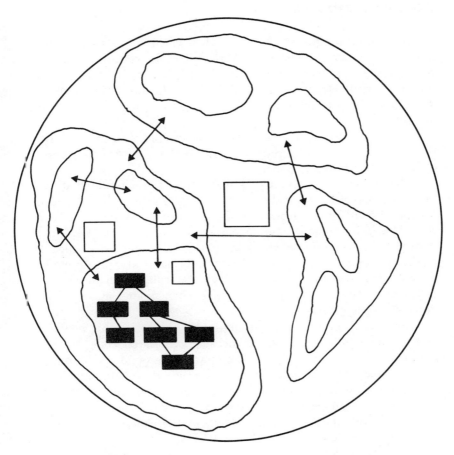

PHASE: Logic design

SUBPHASE: Module logic design

ACTIVITY: Internal logic design of each module

METHODOLOGY: Structured programming logic

OUTPUT: Description of the internal logic of each module. Could be expressed in a
HIPO diagram, second half of the module prologue, APL statements, actual
source statements, or any combination of the above.

FIGURE 8.10.   Module logic design

109

(particularly coupling) are useful in some of the other steps (Figures 8.6 and 8.7).

STRUCTURED PROGRAMMING

Structured programming is a method of coding a program using a limited number of control structures.[5, 18, 20] In concept it is analogous to the approach used in hardware development of building complex circuits from elementary AND, OR, and NOT gates. The three basic structured programming structures are shown in Figure 8.11.

Bohm and Jacopini have shown that any program can be written with these structures.[5] A program written this way has the property of having no statement labels.

If these rules are combined with an additional rule that states that each segment (or module) has exactly one entry point and one exit point, mathematical proof of the program's correctness is simplified. Although proving program correctness is currently beyond the state-of-the-art except for small programs, following these rules dramatically increases a program's clarity. Informational-strength modules do not really violate the single-entry-point rule, since there are no code connections between the multiple entry points in an informational-strength module.

Structured programming significantly improves the readability and maintainability of a module because structured code is literally read from top to bottom. There is no jumping around on the program listing, which is a typical fault of a program containing GO TO statements. Figure 8.12 illustrates this difference by comparing a structured and an unstructured section of code. Structured programming also lends itself to the use of indentation rules, which are illustrated in Figure 8.12.

Composite design and structured programming are compatible and go hand-in-hand. Structured programming is a detailed logic-design and coding technique, and as such it can be used in designing and coding each module that was previously defined by composite design. Note that structured programming, by not using the GO TO, eliminates some potential problems in modules having logical strength or content coupling.

An additional rule in structured programming states that modules should be broken down into segments, a piece of code with 50 or fewer statements that has one entry point and one exit point. This rule,

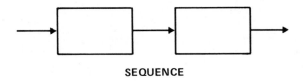

SEQUENCE

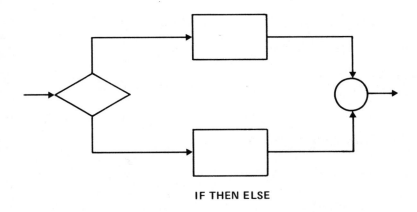

IF THEN ELSE

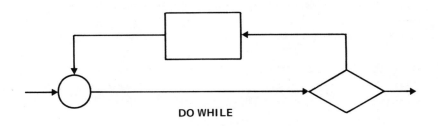

DO WHILE

FIGURE 8.11. Standard programming structures

111

```
        IF p GO TO A          IF p THEN
        IF w GO TO B              F1 function
        F7 function              F2 function
    D:  END MODULE             IF q THEN
    A:  F1 function                        DO WHILE u
        F2 function                            F3 function
        IF q GO TO C                       END DO
        F4 function                    ELSE
    E:  IF NOT v GO TO D                    F4 function
        F5 function            IF v THEN
        GO TO D                             F5 function
    B:  F6 function                     ELSE
        GO TO D            ELSE
    C:  IF NOT u GO TO E        IF w THEN
        F3 function                         F6 function
        GO TO C                         ELSE
                                            F7 function
                          END MODULE
```

FIGURE 8.12.   Unstructured and structured code

although not in conflict with composite design, should not be needed because the modules should already be small enough (see Chapter 5).

TOP-DOWN DEVELOPMENT

Top-down development is an orderly process of approaching the coding and testing of a large program.[3] Coding and testing of the modules begins with the top module in the structure and progresses down through the structure in execution sequence. A top-down development strategy for the simple program in Figure 8.13 begins with modules A and B being coded. "Stubs" (dummy modules) are written to simulate modules C, E, and F. For instance, if the function of module E is "read next command," the stub for module E might be a simple module that returns a wired-in command.

Modules A and B are now tested together using the stubs. Following this the real module E is coded (replacing the stub) and the testing (through module A) is repeated. Next module C is coded and the testing is repeated, still using the stub representing module F. The program is complete when the real module F is coded and testing is repeated.

Note that the program is integrated on a continuous basis and

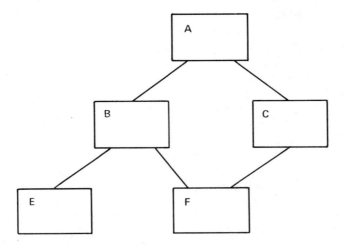

FIGURE 8.13. Top-down versus bottom-up

that all testing proceeds through existing tested parts of the program. The advantages of top-down development are:

1. Integration of the program begins early in the cycle.
2. "Calling" modules are coded before their corresponding "called" (subordinate) modules. Because of this, confusion over module interfaces can be reduced.
3. Test driver code is reduced since each new module is invokable through existing parts of the program.
4. A functioning program becomes available in stages.

Composite design and top-down development are not really related and are therefore compatible. In fact, composite design has also been used successfully with bottom-up development, a strategy discussed in the next section.

BOTTOM-UP DEVELOPMENT

In bottom-up development the order of module coding, testing, and integration begins at the bottom of the structure and proceeds toward the top. Using Figure 8.13 again, modules E and F are coded and tested in parallel. Then modules B and C are coded and tested, using the previously tested E and F. Finally module A is coded and tested, using B, C, E, and F as subordinates.

The premise of bottom-up development is that tested modules become primitive functions that can be built upon. In other words, after module E has been tested, a call to module E should be as reliable as a simple assignment statement.

Bottom-up development has the following advantages:

1. More parallelism can be achieved in the coding and testing phases.
2. Integration begins early in the cycle. However, the major "legs" of the program don't come together until close to the end of the testing cycle.
3. In some situations a more thorough testing job can be done. For instance, in top-down development module E was tested by feeding inputs through module A. It may be difficult to test all paths in E (for example error conditions) using this top-down testing technique.
4. Stubs are not needed. However, tests are driven through each module as opposed to through one module (the top module) in top-down development.

Bottom-up development and top-down development are implementation, not design, strategies. The advantages and disadvantages of each aren't conclusive enough to indicate that one is right and the other is wrong. Because of the second advantage of top-down development (interfaces are verified top-down), it would seem the strategy to use if the validity of the design is questionable. If composite design is used, either top-down or bottom-up development can be used successfully as implementation strategies.

CHIEF PROGRAMMER TEAMS

The chief programmer team is similar in concept to a surgical team in an operating room.[3] The team consists of a chief programmer, a backup programmer, a program librarian, and two to four other programmers. The chief programmer, a highly competent programmer, is the prime designer and also codes the "top" modules in the program. The backup programmer shares the design and implementation work with the chief programmer and can also fill the leadership role of the chief programmer, if required. A third team member, the programming librarian, maintains the documentation and code in a program library system. Other programmers on the team produce the remainder of the code under the close supervision of the chief programmer.

When composite design is used, the program design should be done by one person or, in the case of a large program, by a small number of people. This fits in well with the concept of the chief programmer. For a moderate-sized program the chief programmer should design the structure and then assign detailed module design and coding to the other programmers on the team. For a larger program (involving several programming teams) the structural design should be done by a team of chief programmers who then, after the design is complete, supervise the implementation of the program by each of their teams.

HIPO

Hierarchical Input Process Output (HIPO) is a documentation technique for describing program logic.[16] It is a better technique than flowcharts because HIPO diagrams show data flow through the program as well as logic flow.

As is the case with the other techniques, HIPO and composite design are complementary. After the structural-design step is complete, HIPO diagrams can be used to express the detailed logic design of each module. A HIPO diagram of DEFINE PART, a module in the inventory-control program of Chapter 7, is illustrated in Figure 8.14.

A second aspect of HIPO (the hierarchical part) is a visual table of contents, a diagram somewhat similar to the structural diagram of composite design. The structural diagram is more precise, contains more information, and has better notation (see Appendix) to represent program structure. Hence the composite-design structural diagram should be used instead of the HIPO visual table of contents. The structural diagram can be used in the same fashion as the visual table of contents, that is, as a graphical representation of the program structure to serve as an index for locating the HIPO diagram for any particular module in the program.

MANAGING THE DESIGN PROCESS

Project managers get more nervous in the design stages of a project than in the coding and testing stages because program design is not normally a visible process (managers can see and touch code

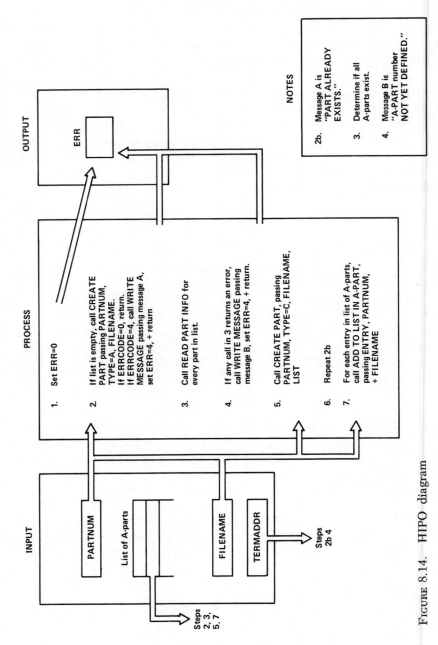

INPUT

PARTNUM

List of A-parts

FILENAME

TERMADDR

→ Steps 2b 4

→ Steps 2, 3, 5, 7

PROCESS

1. Set ERR=0

2. If list is empty, call CREATE PART passing PARTNUM, TYPE=A, FILENAME. If ERRCODE=0, return. If ERRCODE=4, call WRITE MESSAGE passing message A, set ERR=4, + return

3. Call READ PART INFO for every part in list.

4. If any call in 3 returns an error, call WRITE MESSAGE passing message B, set ERR=4, + return.

5. Call CREATE PART, passing PARTNUM, TYPE=C, FILENAME, LIST

6. Repeat 2b

7. For each entry in list of A-parts, call ADD TO LIST IN A-PART, passing ENTRY, PARTNUM, + FILENAME

OUTPUT

ERR

NOTES

2b. Message A is "PART ALREADY EXISTS."

3. Determine if all A-parts exist.

4. Message B is "A-PART number NOT YET DEFINED."

FIGURE 8.14. HIPO diagram

116

and test cases), because design is not normally testable (managers can see the results of testing a piece of code) and because design progress is not normally measurable (managers can count modules as they're coded). Composite design can remove some of this uneasiness.

Composite design helps make the design process more visible simply because it is a methodology to be followed in program design. Because of this the manager understands the end result that the designers are trying to achieve. The design can be evaluated by examining it in terms of strength, coupling, predictability, decision structure, and other factors. The model described in Chapter 10 is a quantitative technique for doing this. Design progress can be measured by examining the partially completed structure diagrams and evaluating how much more work is required to complete the structure. Breaking the total design process into distinct steps, such as those in Figures 8.4 through 8.10, also helps in measuring design progress.

DESIGN REVIEWS

After a structural design has been completed, a formal review process is beneficial. One technique is to take a set of hypothetical inputs to the program and "walk through" the structure.

The first step is to organize the participants—three or four seems to be an optimal number. They should include the person who designed the structure, the person who wrote the external specifications for the program, and one or two other programmers. The purpose of the review is to uncover flaws in the design but not to redesign the program on the fly. To accomplish this, one participant should have the job of taking notes on all problems that are discovered. Correcting these problems becomes the job of the designer after (not during) the review.

Prior to the review charts should be drawn up assuming an initial state of the system and several representative inputs to the program. For instance, to review the inventory-control structure in Chapter 7, a chart might be developed showing a few part records in the data base and a second chart showing a sequence of terminal commands and the expected results for each.

Each input (test variation) is then driven through the design, module by module. Remember that the purpose of the review is to verify the program structure, not the logic of each module. To do this, assume that the logic in each module is correct, that each module performs its function correctly. Look for flaws in the module structure, incomplete interfaces, and incorrect results. During the process update the initial-state chart (for example, the data base records) as the program changes it. It also helps to record the current value of each data item in the program.

As each test variation is being driven through the structure, each participant should be asking himself the following questions:

1. Are the interfaces complete? Does each module receive its necessary input parameters from its callers and its necessary output parameters from its subordinates?
2. Are the interfaces broader than necessary? Are all input parameters from its callers and all output parameters from its subordinate modules either used in the module or passed to another module?
3. Did the program produce the expected results?

In addition the following general questions should be kept in mind:

1. Do all modules have functional strength? If not, ask the designer to explain his reasons.
2. Are all modules strictly data coupled? If not, ask the designer to explain his reasons.
3. Without too much effort, could you visualize the logic of each module? If not, the decomposition may not yet be complete.
4. Are there any instances of unpredictable modules?
5. Does a module directly affect modules that aren't subordinate to it (decision-structure problems)?
6. Does the documentation for any module make it a restrictive module?
7. Has the data access of each module been minimized?
8. Do you know of any existing modules that can be used in this program?

Experience has shown this type of design review to be invaluable. Major flaws in the program can be discovered at an early stage in the program's development at a small cost (only a few man-hours are involved in the review). Also, major improvements in the structural design are often a result.

Similar conclusions were also independently reached at the end of the development of the OS/360 Time Sharing Option (TSO). In the TSO project most of the design testing emphasis was placed on verifying module logic. This emphasis was misplaced because module logic errors are usually more economically corrected by isolated on-line testing of the module (unit testing). The project manager, Dr. A. L. Scherr, concluded that because component and system-level testing occurs late in the cycle, when error correction is most costly, the emphasis in design verification should be placed on ensuring that module interfaces and system flow are correct.[26]

The reason that design reviews of the type described in this section are successful is that a designer may not see what he doesn't want to see. Few people like to find flaws in their own work. Weinberg calls this the principle of cognitive dissonance.[28] Having other people examine and constructively criticize a design gets around this barrier. However, the success of this process is highly dependent on the environment in the programming shop. If the people involved are "egoless programmers," the process will work.[28] If the designer is defensive and protective about his work, the design review will be a wasted effort.

MANAGING THE IMPLEMENTATION PROCESS

Two of the biggest problems facing programming project managers are resource imbalances, which result when programming resources (like programmers) cannot easily be shifted around to match the current workload, and the inability to measure the progress of a project, which results from the lack of small measurable units of work. Composite design can assist in the solution of these problems.

The output of structural-design activity is a structural diagram indicating the relationships among all modules, the function of each module, and definitions of all interfaces. The modules are highly independent and the interfaces are well defined, which reduces misunderstandings and communications problems among programmers during implementation. The modules are small, which makes them more comprehensible and more easily tested (by reducing the total number of logic paths through the modules).

Because of the high independence of the module, programmer assignments can be easily shifted from module to module to smooth out the peaks and valleys in resource requirements. This allows more flexibility in allocating manpower to meet changing conditions. The characteristic of small modules also enhances this smoothing capability. Furthermore, since implementation involves a large number of small modules, more precise planning of programmer workloads is possible.

The second problem mentioned above is the inability to accurately measure the progress of a project. This problem is caused by having too few points of measurement and ambiguously defined points of measurement. Envision a program consisting of one large module. Checkpoints such as "50 percent code written" or "70 percent test cases successful" are usually meaningless. First, they have different meanings to different people. Second, they're misleading, since "70 percent test cases successful" does not imply that 70 percent of the testing effort is complete.

The answer to this problem is measuring progress based on a number of smaller measurable activities, such as the logic design, coding, and testing of small, independent modules.

DOCUMENTATION

The output of the structural-design phase should be a description of the structure of the program (the structural diagram) and a description of the intermodule interfaces. A phase that closely follows this phase (see Figure 8.9) is the external design of each module. The output of this phase is a description of each module in terms of its name, function, inputs, outputs, and external effects. Previous chapters adequately describe the output of the structural-design phase, and the Appendix defines the notation. This section discusses the module's external specifications.

A module should have two types of specifications: an *external module specification*, which describes only that information needed by a module that calls this module, and an *internal module specification*, which describes the internal logic of the module. It is important to distinguish between, and physically separate, these two specifications because the internal module specifications can be altered without affecting the calling modules, but changes to the external module specifications usually require changes to the calling modules.

The internal module specification is written during the implementation process (Figure 8.10) and may take one of several forms. Only the external module specification will be discussed here because of its close relationship with composite design.

The external module specification should describe all of the information needed by the calling modules, and nothing more. Therefore, this specification should describe the module's name, function, inputs, outputs, and external effects.

Module Name

This is a definition of the name that is used (for example, in the CALL statement) to reference the module. Module names should be descriptive of the function performed by the module.

Function

The function performed by the module should be described in a single sentence followed by an expanded description, if necessary. The expanded description could be a narrative description, decision table, graphs, or other similar material. Note that only the module's function, not its internal logic or operation, should be described here.

Inputs

There should be a precise description of all input data to the module. It should include all input parameters, their physical order, their size, their type (e.g., binary, decimal, character), and the range of valid values.

If the module is other than data coupled, input descriptions will be more complex.

Outputs

There should be a precise description of all output data from the module. It should include output parameters and their physical order, size, type, range, and error information (for instance, return codes). If different classes of outputs may be returned, the output should be described in terms of cause-and-effect relationships with the input. Again, if the module is other than data coupled, output descriptions will be more complex.

External Effects

In addition to inputs and outputs modules often have external effects. An external effect is some action taken that manifests itself outside the program (for example, the reading of a tape record or the printing of a report). These actions should be documented as part of the module external specification. If the external effects are conditional, if they don't always occur, they should be related to the inputs in a cause-and-effect manner—to those inputs that cause the effect.

The external effects describe the possible external actions that may occur when this module is called. Because the module external specification is independent of the module's logic, the action could be directly taken by this module or by a subordinate module. In terms of the module external specification, however, any external effect that may possibly occur when this module is called should be part of the module external specification.

Often a module's specifications are found at the beginning of the module in a "module prolog," a group of standard comments statements (for example, in the IDENTIFICATION DIVISION in a COBOL module). The prolog should not indicate which modules call this module. Suppose the prolog of module B states that it is called by module A. Later, if module C is added and it is to call module B, module B has to be altered (to update its prolog), which conflicts with the goal of independence.

Note that although a module's specifications should not reference the calling modules, a module's internal specification will normally describe any calls to other modules from this module. Hence module specifications should describe processing only in that module and any modules that it directly calls; they should make no reference to any other modules. An example of a module external specification is given in Figure 8.15.

The value of documentation has been emphasized for many years (for instance, see reference 6). In addition to the usual reasons (communicating the design to the implementing programmer, maintainability, extensibility) good module documentation is essential to achieving one of the objectives of composite design, the ability to reuse modules in other programs. Accomplishing this requires well-designed modules, well-documented modules, and a mechanism for making this documentation widely available.

PROGRAM EFFICIENCY

Some valid reservations may be raised about the efficiency of a program created by composite design. In certain areas a program designed in this way will contain some overhead that might not have

MODULE NAME: ADDPARTS

FUNCTION: Increment the on-hand amount for specified part

INPUT:	Parameter	Bytes	Type	Range
	1. PARTNUMBER	8	CHAR	Any
	2. NUMBER	4	BINARY	Any (pos or neg)
	3. TERMADDR	4	BINARY	Any
	4. FILENAME	8	CHAR	Any
OUTPUT:	5. ERR	4	BINARY	0, 4, or 8

If 0, funtion performed.
If 4, PARTNUMBER is not an atomic part.
If 8, I/O error.

EXTERNAL EFFECTS:
1. If ERR = 0, data base specified by FILENAME updated (on-hand amount).
2. If ERR = 4, message "VALID ATOMIC PART NOT SPECIFIED" written to terminal specified by TERMADDR.
3. If ERR = 8, message "I/O ERROR — COMMAND DISREGARDED" written to terminal specified by TERMADDR.

NOTE: If TERMADDR = 0, effects 2 and 3 will not occur.

FIGURE 8.15.   Module external specification

been present if the program had been designed in some other way. However, this must be weighed against the development, maintenance, and modification costs and the costs associated with unreliability.

When efficiency is weighed against these other attributes, the issue becomes clouded. For instance, is a program that executes in two seconds but costs $1,000 to change better or worse than an equivalent program that executes in ten seconds but costs $500 to change? Is a system with a steady two-second response time and a mean time to failure of two hours better than a system with a steady four-second response time and a mean time to failure of twenty hours? Moreover, the cost per unit of execution has been decreasing year by year, and the cost per unit of programming has been increasing.

This problem is complicated further because programmers are often concerned with microefficiencies such as squeezing microseconds out of a program's execution time by doing things such as tinkering with module linkages or worrying about whether a subtract instruction or exclusive–or instruction should be used to zero a register. Such practices were needed in the early days when machines were slower and programming was cheaper, but they are no longer appropriate. Today there are more important objectives—decreasing the cost of programming, making programs easier to change and more reliable, and similar issues.

Efficiency is still important today, but it should be approached in terms of macroefficiencies. Today's programmers should be oriented toward such improvements in efficiency as reducing the storage used by a program (important in a virtual-memory environment), reducing the number of accesses to a data base, reducing the time that a resource is tied up, and input/output buffering.

To demonstrate that the intention here is not to dodge the efficiency question completely, four factors of execution speed will be examined—source-code efficiency, execution overhead, memory usage, and resource usage.

Source-code efficiency is the efficiency of the code generated by the programmer. Composite design should have no effect on this, although composite design can make source-code optimization easier, which will be discussed in a moment.

Execution overhead is the execution time added due to the presence of code not directly generated by the programmer. This normally manifests itself in code generated by the compiler for intermodule linkages like CALL statements. Because composite design generates a larger number of relatively small modules, execution overhead may be increased. The significance of this varies depending on the mechanism used by the compiler, the architecture of the computer that the program will operate on, the frequency of calls, and in some cases the number of parameters passed.

In addition, code optimization algorithms in certain optimizing compilers do not function properly if the module is over a certain size. Composite design, because of its emphasis on small modules, allows full compiler code optimization to occur. Very often this outweighs any overhead caused by CALL statements.

In a virtual-memory environment the way in which a program uses memory and the way the program is packaged into memory are significant execution-time factors. Composite design is advantageous in this environment because it allows more flexibility in packaging the program's modules in an optimal fashion. Chapter 9 discusses this in more detail. Certain programming languages such as PL/I dynamically allocate storage for data used in the program. Using smaller modules reduces the average amount of storage allocated, since only those modules that are currently activated have this storage allocated.

Resource usage is the number and duration of resources used by the program. A resource can be a file, terminal, printer, etc. (The central processing unit and memory are also resources, but these were discussed in the previous paragraphs). Composite design has no effect on resource usage.

The best way to improve execution speed is to study the program, determine the places where the most execution time is being spent, and optimize those places. This is much different from the usual practice of "local optimization," where a programmer spends several manweeks optimizing an error-handling module that executes for seven milliseconds every four days. Composite design aids global optimization by allowing the program to be initially developed in a shorter period of time. The working program can then be measured to locate the critical modules. The results are very often surprising. The critical modules often turn out to be ones that were not suspected. Then, because of high module independence, these modules can be optimized and reintegrated into the program without introducing multitudes of errors into the rest of the program.

OTHER HINTS

Completing the entire structural design process before any coding starts is a necessity. As was pointed out in Chapter 6, design is an iterative process, and several passes through the structure are usually necessary. Writing the first line of code appears to raise a psychological barrier to any design improvements. Because the chance to improve the structural design has a larger long-range benefit than starting coding a few weeks early, coding should be delayed until several iterations have been made through the structural-design process.

It is very easy to destroy a well-designed program with just a couple of careless modifications. Of course, it's even easier to destroy a poorly designed program. This exposure is the highest in program-maintenance activities. When a bug is found, there is a temptation to correct it in the easiest and quickest way possible. The project manager must avoid giving programmers this temptation, since a quick and dirty fix may correct the current problem but may also degrade the design of the program, resulting in more bugs and higher maintenance and modification costs in the future. To help in avoiding this problem, program maintainers should be educated in composite design. If the maintainers have a clear understanding of the design objectives of the program, they will take pride in making sure that their changes meet (or even exceed) these objectives.

CHAPTER 9

MODULARITY AND VIRTUAL STORAGE

The concept of virtual storage is heralded as a means to make the programmer's job easier and more productive, since it lessens the problems of designing for a particular memory size, packaging a program into overlays, etc. These claims are certainly valid. However, to ensure adequate performance, the programmer must now worry about the effects of paging on his program.

Performance in a paging environment is inversely related to the number of page faults incurred. A page fault is the interruption that occurs when a reference is made to part of the program (a page of virtual memory) that is not currently in real memory. Because of this, the programmer should attempt to find an optimal packaging of his program and data, a packaging that minimizes the number of page faults. Experiments in this area have shown that proper packaging can result in as much as a five-to-one reduction in the number of page faults. For good introductions to virtual storage see references 11 and 17.

Throughout this book there are repeated warnings against thinking about the procedural aspects of the program. There will be no such warnings in this chapter because packaging of a program in a paging environment is entirely a procedural problem; that is, it is based on the execution characteristics of the program.

To package a program in a paging environment, the following information is needed: the size of a page (assuming the system has a single fixed page size); the size of each module in the program; a structural diagram of the program; and some knowledge of the procedural aspects of the program, in particular the when and why behind the calls to each module. This process involves the proper physical placement of modules among pages within the virtual storage to minimize page faults. Since packaging is a procedural problem and since it requires the output of the design phase, it cannot be considered during the design phase. Because packaging requires knowledge of each module's physical size, it cannot normally be considered until after the coding phase.

Packaging is primarily an art. Several prioritized guidelines will be discussed and then illustrated in an example.

PRIORITY 1: ITERATIONS

Group together modules that call one another iteratively. In Figure 9.1, if module A iteratively calls module B, then A and B should be grouped together in the same page.

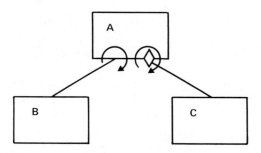

FIGURE 9.1.   Iterative calls

Probability of execution is another factor. If A repeatedly calls B and C and it repeatedly calls B every time A is executed but repeatedly calls C only sometimes, then A grouped with B is of top priority and A grouped with C is of lesser priority.

PRIORITY 2: HIGH FAN-IN

Groups of modules with a high fan-in (number of calling modules) that are called by the same set of modules—should be grouped together. In Figure 9.2, if A and B are called by a set of modules (C, D, and E), then A and B should be grouped together.

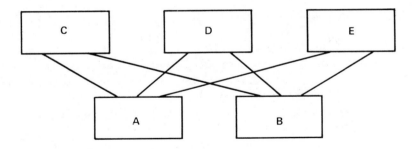

FIGURE 9.2. High fan-in

PRIORITY 3: FREQUENCY

Group together those modules that call one another most frequently. For instance, in Figure 9.3 A calls B every time A is executed, A calls C about 50 percent of the time, and A calls D infrequently. The first concern should be to group A and B together. Grouping A and C (and B) together is of lesser importance but desirable if possible. Grouping A and D together should probably be avoided.

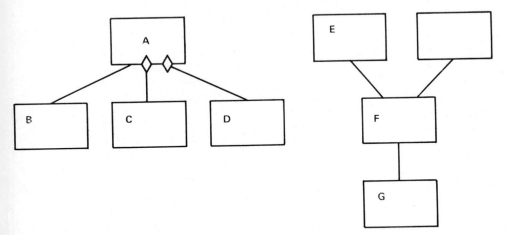

FIGURE 9.3. Frequency of calls

Also in Figure 9.3, if a choice must be made to group E and F together or F and G together, the latter is of higher priority because the F–G call is more frequent than the E–F call.

PRIORITY 4: EXECUTION SEQUENCE

If the above three priorities have been exhausted and space still exists within the pages for additional modules, execution sequence should be the next consideration. Modules that execute sequentially should be grouped together as much as possible.

Consider the diagram in Figure 9.4; for this example, assume the execution sequence is:

ABFBGBACADAEHEIEA

Assume that any five of these modules can be fit on one page and the other four on another page. The solution is obtained by scanning the execution sequence and picking any sequence of five unique names. For instance, if the first five unique names in the sequence are picked, A, B, F, G, and C will be in the first page and D, E, H, and I will be in the second page. This yields four potential page faults in the execution, two in the call of D from A and the return to A, and two in the call of E from A and the return to A.

In fact, any five modules together in the sequence could be chosen. For instance, starting at position 4, B, G, A, C, and D could be chosen for one page, which still yields four potential page faults. If this is done without considering the execution sequence, the number of page faults is greater. For instance, placing A, B, C, F, and H in one page yields eight potential page faults. Placing A, B, C, D, and E in one page also yields eight potential page faults.

Even when the execution sequence cannot be determined (if, for instance, decisions in the modules alter the execution sequence), this technique can be used by determining the most probable execution sequence.

PRIORITY 5: LOCATION IN STRUCTURE

When using the above four priorities, one may end up trying to group more modules on a page than space will allow (the sum of the size of the grouped modules may be greater than the page size). To resolve this, take the modules in the lower positions in the hierarchy and group those together first. The reason for this is that module calls toward the bottom of the hierarchy tend to be executed more frequently than module calls toward the top of the structure.

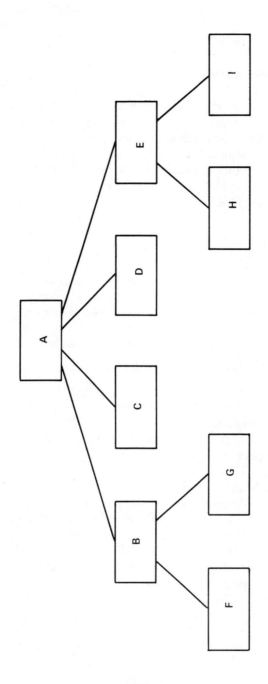

FIGURE 9.4. Execution sequence

131

NONGROUPING CRITERIA

In addition to the above guidelines for grouping modules on pages there are several cases where certain modules shouldn't be grouped together. Not grouping modules of this sort together will allow more freedom to make additional desirable groupings.

Any module that is executed only once should be separated from its caller. Any modules that perform infrequently used optional functions should also be separated from their callers.

EXAMPLE

The diagram in Figure 9.5 will be used as an example. The module sizes are indicated in the lower-right-hand corners of each module. Assume that the page size is 1,000 bytes.

The first step is to find priority-1 groupings. By examining the iterations, the following three groups are obtained:

(B D E F G H)   (D L)   (C I J K)

The next step is to find priority-2 groups. Modules R, S, T, and U meet the criteria since they are called by a common set of modules. Therefore the single priority-2 group is (R S T U).

Priority-3 groups are now developed. Making a few assumptions about the program, two groups of high-frequency calls are found. They are (R T U N O P) and (P J).

The fourth and fifth priorities will be skipped for the time being and returned to later if the first three priorities are insufficient.

Start by packaging modules together in the first priority-1 group (B D E F G H). Their combined size is 1,250 bytes. Something has to be omitted, so B, D, E, F, and H (750 bytes) are placed on page 1 and G on page 2. The next group is D and L. Since D is on page 1, L can be included on page 1 for a total of 800 bytes.

The next priority-1 group is (C I J K). Since they cannot fit on pages 1 or 2, they are placed on page 3 (combined total of 700 bytes).

The only priority-2 group is (R S T U). Since this cannot fit on the first three pages, it is placed on page 4 (600 bytes).

There are two priority-3 groups. The first group has a size of 1,500 bytes, so it can't be placed intact on page 4. Since the second priority-3 group also contains P, modules P and J will be placed on a

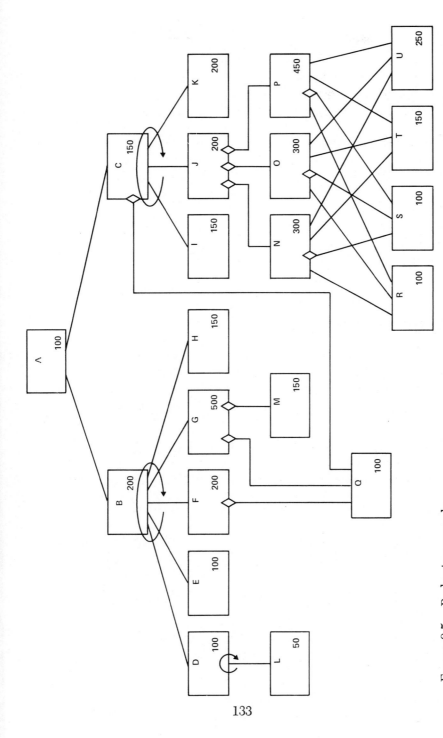

FIGURE 9.5. Packaging example

133

new page, page 5. The (R T U N O) group is still too large (1,100 bytes), so N or O must be removed. If O is removed and placed on page 5, page 4 now contains 900 bytes and page 5 contains 950 bytes.

The three remaining modules are A, M, and Q. Page 2 currently contains module G, and since modules Q and M are connected to G in execution sequence, M and Q are placed in page 2. A should go in pages 1 or 3. Since page 3 currently has more empty space than page 1, A is placed in page 3.

The packaging is:

Page 1:   B D E F H L
Page 2:   G M Q
Page 3:   C I K J A
Page 4:   R S T U N
Page 5:   O P J

EXPERIMENTATION

Now that a way of packaging a particular program has been determined, further optimization is probably worthwhile. For instance, make sure that the program is packaged in a minimum number of pages (the pages shouldn't have a lot of blank space). The following optimizing procedure is suggested:

1. Pick one or more most probable executions of the program.
2. For these cases write down the execution sequences by module.
3. Make an assumption about the number of page frames in real storage available to the program (assume it's a constant). That is, assume the program will always have n pages in real storage.
4. Walk each of the execution sequences from step 2 through the program. On paper (and in your mind) perform the paging and count the number of page faults. Use either the paging algorithm of the system that this program will execute on or assume a paging strategy—for example, demand paging with replacement of the least recently used page.
5. Now make a change to the packaging. For instance, if some arbitrary decisions were made in the original packaging, try an alternative. Repeat step 4 and compare the results (number of page faults).

Note that although this procedure can be used to optimize module packaging, it does not give a completely accurate indication of the actual paging that will occur when the program is executing. Paging is dependent on such additional factors as: how the compiler allocates storage for variables, save areas, and parameter lists; how many times your program calls the operating system for such services as storage allocation and input/output; and the fact that many programs are competing for pages of real storage. However, most of these factors cannot be controlled by the programmer.

This chapter has described an art, not an exact science. For a more sophisticated technique involving the examination of the reference patterns of a program, see reference 15.

CHAPTER 10

A MODEL OF
PROGRAM STABILITY

Module independence is primarily affected by module strength and module coupling. Because of this, a quantitative measure of the independence of two modules could be developed based on some quantitative relationship of the strength of the two modules and the coupling between them. Once this is obtained, a model could be developed for the entire program, using probability and graph theory. Such a model, the subject of this chapter, could be used to predict the stability of the program (and thus the ramifications of changing the program).

Suppose there was a matrix describing the dependence among all of the modules in a program. For the moment don't be concerned with how the matrix was obtained. Such a matrix might look like Figure 10.1.

This matrix describes the probability of having to change module i, given that module j must be changed. For instance, if module A is changed, there is a 30-percent chance that module B must be changed.

The major portion of this chapter is concerned with the development of this matrix. Assuming that the matrix is already available, however, the following things could be done with it:

1. Sum up all of the elements in the matrix and divide by five (the dimension of the matrix). This number is a measure of the design of the program (the lower the number, the better the design). This number is also the expected number of modules that must be changed when any single module is changed.

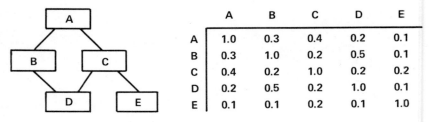

	A	B	C	D	E
A	1.0	0.3	0.4	0.2	0.1
B	0.3	1.0	0.2	0.5	0.1
C	0.4	0.2	1.0	0.2	0.2
D	0.2	0.5	0.2	1.0	0.1
E	0.1	0.1	0.2	0.1	1.0

FIGURE 10.1.   Dependence matrix

In this example the number is 1.92. This implies that the expected number of modules that must be changed when any single module is changed is 1.92 (the module itself plus .92 other modules).

2. Sum up all of the elements in any row i in the matrix. This sum is the expected number of modules that must be changed when module i is changed. For instance, the number for module D is 2.0; the number for module E is 1.5.

3. Sort the elements in any row i by value. This gives a list (in order of probability) of the modules that may have to be changed if module i is changed. The value of such a list should be obvious. For instance, if module D is changed, there is a good chance (0.5) that B will have to be changed, a small chance (0.2) that A or C will have to be changed, and a very small chance (0.1) that E will have to be changed.

The matrix in Figure 10.1 is called a *complete dependence matrix*, which describes all dependencies among all modules.

FIRST-ORDER DEPENDENCE MATRIX

The first process in deriving the complete dependence matrix is to derive the first-order dependence matrix. The first-order dependence matrix defines all first-order dependencies among all modules in the program.

The first-order dependence matrix is derived using the following three steps:

1. Evaluate the coupling among all of the modules in the program. Construct an $m \times m$ coupling matrix, where m is the number of modules in the program. Using Table 10.1, fill in each element

in matrix C. Element C_{ij} represents the coupling between module i and module j.

Table 10.1   Module Coupling

Coupling	Value
Content	.95
Common	.7
External	.6
Control	.5
Stamp	.35
Data	.2

Note that the matrix is symmetric, that is,

$$C_{ij} = C_{ji}$$

for all i and j. Also, the elements on the diagonal are all one ($C_{ii} = 1$ for all i).

2. Evaluate the strength of each module in the program. Using Table 10.2, record the corresponding numerical values in vector S (a vector of m elements).

Table 10.2   Module Strength

Strength	Value
Coincidental	.95
Logical	.4
Classical	.6
Procedural	.4
Communicational	.25
Informational	.2
Functional	.2

3. Construct the first-order dependence matrix D by the formula:

$$D_{ij} = 0.15(S_i + S_j) + 0.7C_{ij} \text{ where } C_{ij} \neq 0$$
$$D_{ij} = 0 \text{ where } C_{ij} = 0$$
$$D_{ii} = 1 \text{ for all } i$$

To illustrate these steps, consider the structure in Figure 10.2. Assume A and B, A and C, A and D, B and E, and C and E are data coupled, C and D are stamp coupled, and D and F are external coupled. Also assume that module E has procedural strength and all others have functional strength. The coupling matrix C and strength vector S are shown in Figure 10.3.

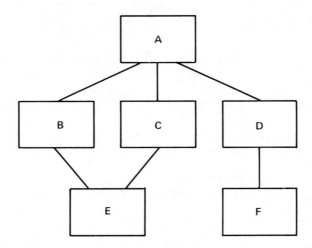

FIGURE 10.2.   Example

The resultant first-order dependence matrix D is shown in Figure 10.4. Note that this matrix can also be pictured as an undirected graph, where the modules are represented by nodes and the edges represent the nonzero matrix elements (first-order dependencies).

The graph is related in some degree to the module structure. If stamp, common, external, and content coupling are absent, the graph is directly analogous to the module structure. Note that in the previous example modules C and D were stamp coupled. Hence the graph in Figure 10.4 contains an edge between C and D.

The first-order dependence matrix is only the first step; it does not tell the entire story. In the above example the probability that module B will change if A changes is not simply 0.2. A change in module A may cause a change in C, which may cause a change

	A	B	C	D	E	F			
A	1.0	0.2	0.2	0.2	0.0	0.0		A	0.2
B	0.2	1.0	0.0	0.0	0.2	0.0		B	0.2
C	0.2	0.0	1.0	0.35	0.2	0.0		C	0.2
D	0.2	0.0	0.35	1.0	0.0	0.6		D	0.2
E	0.0	0.2	0.2	0.0	1.0	0.0		E	0.4
F	0.0	0.0	0.0	0.6	0.0	1.0		F	0.2

FIGURE 10.3.   C matrix and S vector

	A	B	C	D	E	F
A	1.0	0.2	0.2	0.2	0.0	0.0
B	0.2	1.0	0.0	0.0	0.23	0.0
C	0.2	0.0	1.0	0.305	0.23	0.0
D	0.2	0.0	0.305	1.0	0.0	0.48
E	0.0	0.23	0.23	0.0	1.0	0.0
F	0.0	0.0	0.0	0.48	0.0	1.0

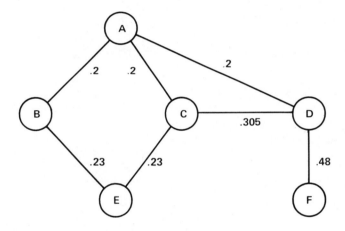

FIGURE 10.4.   First-order dependence matrix

in E, which may cause a change in B. Also, the matrix implies that there is no dependence between A and F, for example. Obviously there is some dependence among all modules in a program. The next section, which shows the derivation of the complete dependence matrix, will resolve these problems.

COMPLETE DEPENDENCE MATRIX

To understand the difference between the first-order dependence matrix and the complete dependence matrix, consider the first-order dependence matrix in Figure 10.5.

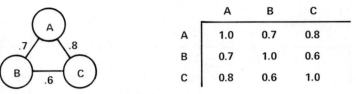

	A	B	C
A	1.0	0.7	0.8
B	0.7	1.0	0.6
C	0.8	0.6	1.0

FIGURE 10.5.   Simple first-order dependence matrix

Assume module A must be changed and determine the probability of having to change B. Let x represent the event of changing B directly because of a change in A (first-order dependence). Let y represent the event of changing B because A causes a change in C. The probability of x, $P(x)$, is 0.7; $P(y) = 0.48$ (0.8×0.6). The events represented by x and y are not mutually exclusive, hence their probabilities cannot simply be added. The formula that must be used is:

$$P(B \text{ changing}) = P(X) + P(Y) - P(X)P(Y)$$

$$= 0.7 + 0.48 - (0.7)(0.48)$$

$$= 0.844$$

Carrying this out for all combinations leads to the complete dependence matrix in Figure 10.6.

	A	B	C
A	1.0	0.844	0.884
B	0.844	1.0	0.824
C	0.884	0.824	1.0

FIGURE 10.6.   Resulting complete dependence matrix

Unfortunately, most programs are much more complicated than this. Consider a slightly more complicated example in Figure 10.7.

Assuming A must change, there are three possible chances of B changing (that is, three unique paths to B, A–B, A–C–B, and A–C–D–B). Call these three events x, y, and z.

$$P(x) = 0.4$$

$$P(y) = 0.3 \times 0.4 = 0.12$$

$$P(z) = 0.3 \times 0.2 \times 0.5 = 0.03$$

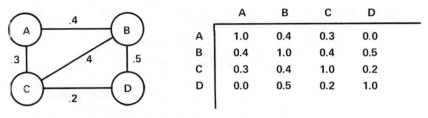

	A	B	C	D
A	1.0	0.4	0.3	0.0
B	0.4	1.0	0.4	0.5
C	0.3	0.4	1.0	0.2
D	0.0	0.5	0.2	1.0

FIGURE 10.7. Another first-order dependence matrix

Because these three events are not mutually exclusive, the following formula must be used:

$$P(\text{B changing}) = P(x) + P(y) + P(z) - P(x)P(y)$$
$$- P(y)P(z) - P(x)P(z) + P(x)P(y)P(z)$$
$$= 0.48784$$

The problem of deriving the complete dependence matrix is now becoming increasingly complex (and nonlinearly so). The problem is twofold: Finding all possible paths in the first-order dependence matrix between every pair of modules, and computing the probabilities between every pair of modules.

The problem will be simplified (yielding an approximate solution) by selecting, from the set of paths between two modules, the three paths with the highest probabilities. Loops within the graph are not considered. For instance, the path A–B–C is a valid path between A and C, but A–B–C–D–B–C is not a valid path

The general procedure for deriving the complete dependence matrix is:

1. Find all paths between module i and module j. The probability of a path is the product of all of the edges in that path.
2. If there is only one path,

$$E_{ij} = E_{ji} = P(x),$$

where $P(x)$ is the path probability.
3. If there are two paths,

$$E_{ij} = E_{ji} = P(x) + P(y) - P(x)P(y)$$

where $P(x)$ and $P(y)$ are the two path probabilities.

4. If there are three or more paths, find the three paths with the highest probabilities. Call these $P(x)$, $P(y)$, and $P(z)$. Then,

$$E_{ij} = E_{ji} = P(x) + P(y) + P(z) - P(x)P(y)$$
$$- P(x)P(z) - P(y)P(z) + P(x)P(y)P(z)$$

For any but a very small program, the complete-dependence matrix cannot be derived easily by paper and pencil. APL programs have been written to perform the computations.[21] The programs accept the coupling and strength descriptions as input and produce the complete-dependence matrix.

USING THE COMPLETE DEPENDENCE MATRIX

The complete dependence matrix appears to be a valuable description of a program. Four uses of the complete dependence matrix, overall design measure, expected change measure, zero-change measure, and module relationships are considered here.

Overall Design Measure

Summing all of the elements in the complete dependence matrix and dividing this sum by the number of modules (the dimension of the matrix) yields a number that is an overall measure of the independence of the program. The number is inversely proportional to the independence of the parts of the program and is actually the expected number of modules that must be changed, given that a random module is changing.

Expected Change Measure

Summing the elements in row i yields the expected number of modules that must be changed, given that module i is changing. Such a list indicates the independence of each module in the program. This list can be used as a measure of individual modules and as a method to evaluate the consequences of a design change or a program-error fix.

Zero-Change Measure

The complete dependence matrix can be used to compute the probability of no other modules having to change, given that module *i* is changing. To find this, subtract each element in row *i* from 1.0 (omit the *i*th element) and then sum these numbers together.

List of Related Modules

By sorting the elements in row *i* by value, a list is obtained (in order of dependence) of modules related to module *i*. This list could be used to provide answers to such questions as:

1. If module *i* is changing, what other modules should be examined? In other words, what other modules have a high probability of changing?
2. If module *i* is changing, what is the best selection of other modules that should be retested in order to verify that the program hasn't regressed?

EXAMPLE

The model will be used on the program shown in Figure 10.8. All modules have functional strength except module 3, which has procedural strength, and module 10, which has classical strength. All interfaces shown use data coupling. In addition modules 4, 8, and 9 share a nonglobal data area (stamp coupling), and modules 3 and 4 have external coupling.

Figure 10.9 contains the resultant complete dependence matrix. An examination of the top row indicates that, if module 1 is changing, there is a 21 percent chance of module 2 having to change, a 32 percent chance of module 3 having to change, and so on. Note the close relationship between modules 3 and 4 (0.53) and the remote connection between, for instance, modules 11 and 12 (0.0). The value is really nonzero (0.000252), but all values less than 0.005 are indicated as zero.

Table 10.3 contains the expected number of other modules that must be changed, given that a particular module is changing. For instance, if module 8 is changing, the model predicts that 1.49 other modules will have to change. This table gives a good indication of module independence. Module 11 is the most independent, and module 4 is the least. The overall independence measure of the program is 1.1. In other words, given that a random module must change, the expected number of other modules that will require change is 1.1.

Table 10.4 contains another view of the program, the probability

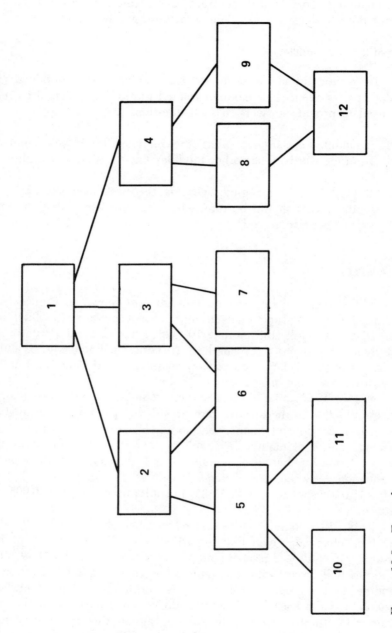

146

Figure 10.8. Example

	1	2	3	4	5	6	7	8	9	10	11	12
1	1.00	0.21	0.32	0.30	0.04	0.11	0.08	0.11	0.11	0.01	0.01	0.03
2	0.21	1.00	0.11	0.08	0.20	0.21	0.03	0.03	0.03	0.05	0.04	0.01
3	0.32	0.11	1.00	0.53	0.02	0.24	0.23	0.21	0.21	0.01	0.00	0.07
4	0.30	0.08	0.53	1.00	0.02	0.13	0.13	0.38	0.38	0.00	0.00	0.14
5	0.04	0.20	0.02	0.02	1.00	0.04	0.01	0.01	0.01	0.26	0.20	0.00
6	0.11	0.21	0.24	0.13	0.04	1.00	0.06	0.05	0.05	0.01	0.01	0.02
7	0.08	0.03	0.23	0.13	0.01	0.06	1.00	0.05	0.05	0.00	0.00	0.02
8	0.11	0.03	0.21	0.38	0.01	0.05	0.05	1.00	0.40	0.00	0.00	0.26
9	0.11	0.03	0.21	0.38	0.01	0.05	0.05	0.40	1.00	0.00	0.00	0.26
10	0.01	0.05	0.01	0.00	0.26	0.01	0.00	0.00	0.00	1.00	0.05	0.00
11	0.01	0.04	0.00	0.00	0.20	0.01	0.00	0.00	0.00	0.05	1.00	0.00
12	0.03	0.01	0.07	0.14	0.00	0.02	0.02	0.26	0.26	0.00	0.00	1.00

FIGURE 10.9.   Complete dependence matrix

Table 10.3   Expected Number of Changes

Changing Module	Expected Number of Other Changed Modules
1	1.33
2	0.99
3	1.94
4	2.09
5	0.80
6	0.93
7	0.64
8	1.49
9	1.49
10	0.40
11	0.32
12	0.80

that no other modules have to change, given that a particular module is changing. If module 4 changes, there is only a 7 percent chance that no other module must change. If module 5 changes, there is a 41 percent chance that no other module must change. Hence if a programmer stated that he fixed a bug in module 4 and didn't have to change any other modules, you should get an uncomfortable feeling. He may be right, but the odds aren't in his favor.

These results give valuable insight into the stability of the program. They help predict the consequences of change and the

Table 10.4   Probability of No Other Changes

Changing Module	Probability That No Other Module Must Be Changed
1	0.22
2	0.34
3	0.09
4	0.07
5	0.41
6	0.36
7	0.50
8	0.17
9	0.17
10	0.64
11	0.71
12	0.41

independence of various parts of the program. For instance, if two programmers are making changes (fixing bugs or adding new function) in modules 4 and 10, they can probably work in isolation (the dependence is less than 0.005). However, if one is changing module 4 and the other is changing module 3 (the dependence is 0.53), they had better talk to one another!

VALIDITY OF THE MODEL

This model has not been empirically derived; it is a theoretical model based mainly on intuition. The equation to compute the first-order dependence matrix is a linear equation based on the values of strength and coupling. The equation was made linear simply because there was no reason to do otherwise. The two factors in the equation (0.15 and 0.7) are educated guesses, based on the reasoning that, in terms of module dependencies, coupling is more of a factor than strength.

Tables 10.1 and 10.2 are also based on educated guesses. One quirk in Table 10.2 is the value associated with logical strength. The reason that logical strength falls out of line is that most of the problems associated with logical strength are within the module and thus do not cause intermodule problems.

One basic premise in the model is the fact that the matrix is symmetric (and that the graph is undirected). This implies that if a change in module A means that there is a 40 percent chance of module B having to change, then the reverse is true, that a change in B means that there is a 40 percent chance of A having to change. At this time there is no reason to disbelieve this premise.

All of these aspects of the model must be verified and refined based on data collected with these purposes in mind. Unfortunately, the proper historical data to validate the model is not readily available. Data collected on bugs in modules and the total number of modules changed because of fixes for the bugs is, even when available, not the proper data. The reason for this is that fixes are often incomplete, since the programmer overlooks some of the implications of the fix.

Models of program structure have been proposed before, although the problem of obtaining input values on the program structure has remained largely unsolved. For instance, Haney defined a related model based on a matrix algebra solution.[14] The composite design measures of module strength and coupling appear to solve the problem of obtaining meaningful inputs to a program structure model.

APPENDIX. NOTATION

The notation for the structure diagrams is shown in Figures A.1, A.2, and A.3. Figure A.1 illustrates the set of notation normally required. Figure A.2 shows an additional set of notation that is procedurally oriented. This additional notation is not necessary, but its use in the structure diagram often adds clarity to the design. Figure A.3 shows an additional specialized set of notation oriented toward operating systems or programs that communicate with their underlying operating system. These symbols are particularly useful in showing which modules contain input/output operations.

In addition any meaningful combinations of this notation can be used.

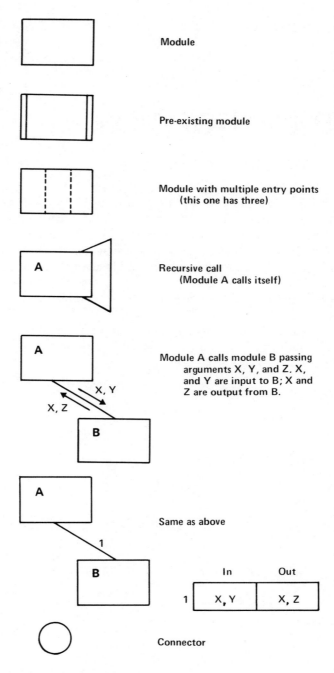

Module

Pre-existing module

Module with multiple entry points
(this one has three)

Recursive call
(Module A calls itself)

Module A calls module B passing
arguments X, Y, and Z. X,
and Y are input to B; X and
Z are output from B.

Same as above

Connector

FIGURE A.1.   Normal notation

152

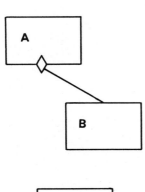

Conditional call. Module A
   sometimes (not always) calls
   module B.

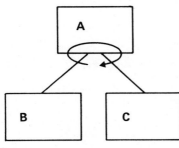

Repetitive call. Module A iterates
   through calls to B and C.

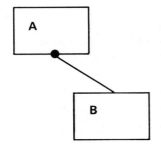

Module A transfers control (without
   return) to module B. In other
   words, a GO TO between modules.
   Not recommended.

FIGURE A.2.   Procedurally oriented notation

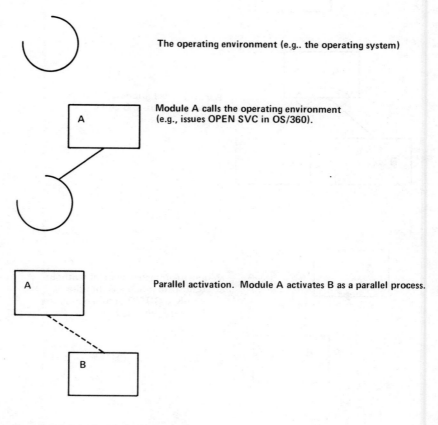

The operating environment (e.g.. the operating system)

Module A calls the operating environment
(e.g., issues OPEN SVC in OS/360).

Parallel activation. Module A activates B as a parallel process.

FIGURE A.3.   Special notation

154

REFERENCES

1. Alexander, C. *Notes on the Synthesis of Form*. Cambridge, Mass.: Harvard University Press, 1964.

2. Ashenhurst, R. L., ed. "Curriculum Recommendations for Graduate Professional Programs in Information Systems," *Communications of the ACM*, Vol. 15, No. 5, 363–398 (May 1972).

3. Baker, F. T. "Chief Programmer Team Management of Production Programming," *IBM Systems Journal*, Vol. 11, No. 1, 56–73 (1972).

4. Belady, L. A., and Lehman, M. M. "Programming System Dynamics or the Metadynamics of Systems in Maintenance and Growth," RC 3546, IBM Thomas J. Watson Research Center, Yorktown Heights, N.Y., 1971, p. 3, p. 8.

5. Bohm, C., and Jacopini, G. "Flow Diagrams, Turing Machines, and Languages with only Two Formation Rules," *Communications of the ACM*, Vol. 9, No. 5, 366–371 (May 1966).

6. Chapin, N. *Flowcharts*. New York: Mason & Lipscomb, 1971.

7. Couger, J. D., ed. "Curriculum Recommendations for Undergraduate Programs in Information Systems," *Communications of the ACM*, Vol. 16, No. 12, 727–749 (December 1973).

8. Constantine, L. L. *Fundamentals of Program System Design*. Unpublished manuscript, 1971.

9. Constantine, L. L., Myers, G. J., and Stevens, W. P. "Structured Design," *IBM Systems Journal*, Vol. 13, No. 2, 115–139 (May 1974).

10. *"Curriculum 68*: Recommendations for Academic Programs in Computer Science. A Report of the ACM Curriculum Committee on Computer Science," *Communications of the ACM*, Vol. 11, No. 3, 151–197 (March 1968).

11. Denning, P. J. "Virtual Memory," *Computing Surveys*, Vol. 2, No. 3, 153–189 (September 1970).

12. Ferdinand, A. E. "Quality in Programming," IBM Systems Development Division, Kingston, N.Y., 1972.

13. Hamming, R. W. "One Man's View of Computer Science," *Journal of the ACM*, Vol. 16, No. 1, 3–12 (January 1969), p. 10.

14. Haney, F. M., "Module Connection Analysis—A Tool for Scheduling Software Debugging Activities," *Proceedings of the 1972 Fall Joint Computer Conference*, Vol. 41, Part 1, 173–179 (1972).

15. Hatfield, D. J., and Gerald, J. "Program Restructuring for Virtual Memory," *IBM Systems Journal*, Vol. 10, No. 3, 168–192 (1971).

16. *HIPO: Design Aid Documentation Tool—Audio Tape*, SR20-9413, IBM Data Processing Division, White Plains, N.Y.

17. *Introduction to Virtual Storage in System/370*, GR20-4260, IBM Data Processing Division, White Plains, N.Y., 1972.

18. Marcus, R., Weinberg, G., and Yasukawa, N. *Structured Programming in PL/C*. New York: John Wiley and Sons, 1973.

19. McGonagle, J. D. "A Study of a Software Development Project," Final Report Contract No. F04701-71-C-0373, James P. Anderson and Co., Fort Washington, Pa., 1971, p. 8.

20. Mills, H., "Top Down Programming in Large Systems," in R. Rustin, ed., *Debugging Techniques in Large Systems*. Englewood Cliffs, N.J.: Prentice-Hall, 1971.

21. Myers, G. J. "A Model for Predicting Program Change," TR 00.2491, IBM System Development Division, Poughkeepsie, N.Y., 1973.

22. Myers, G. J. "Characteristics of Composite Design," *Datamation*, Vol. 19, No. 9, 100–102 (September 1973).

23. Myers, G. J. "Estimating the Costs of a Programming System Development Project," TR 00.2316, IBM Systems Development Division, Poughkeepsie, N.Y., 1972.

24. Ogdin, J. L. "Designing Reliable Software," *DATAMATION*, Vol. 18, No. 7, 71–78 (July 1972).

25. Parnas, D. L. "On the Criteria to Be Used in Decomposing Systems into Modules," *Communications of the ACM*, Vol. 15, No. 12, 1053–1058 (December 1972).

26. Scherr, A. L. "Developing and Testing a Large Programming System, OS/360 Time Sharing Option," in W. C. Hetzel, ed., *Program Test Methods*. Englewood Cliffs, N.J.: Prentice-Hall, 1973.

27. Weinberg, G. M. *PL/I Programming: A Manual of Style*. New York: McGraw Hill, 1970.

28. Weinberg, G. M. *The Psychology of Computer Programming.* New York: Van Nostrand Reinhold, 1971.

INDEX